Mobilizing the C-Suite

Mobilizing the C-Suite

Waging War Against Cyberattacks

Frank Riccardi, JD, CHC

BUSINESS EXPERT PRESS

Leader in applied, concise business books

First published in 2023 by
Business Expert Press, LLC
222 East 46th Street, New York, NY 10017
www.businessexpertpress.com

ISBN-13: 978-1-63742-424-7 (paperback)
ISBN-13: 978-1-63742-425-4 (e-book)

Business Expert Press Business Law and Corporate Risk Management Collection

First edition: 2023

10 9 8 7 6 5 4 3 2 1

To Rosa,
For 23 years of marriage, whiskey nights on the patio,
and countless walks with Lucy and Daisy in the rain.

Description

Cyberattacks are worse now than ever before. Cybercriminals are on the prowl and ready to go full-on goblin mode, shuttering a gas pipeline, switching off an electrical grid, or transmuting credit cards into useless scraps of plastic. To defeat cybercriminals, companies must focus on the low-hanging fruits of cybersecurity. It's all about the basics. Companies laid low by ransomware failed to practice good cyber hygiene by recklessly allowing weak or reused passwords, not turning on multifactor authentication, or neglecting to install patches to known software vulnerabilities.

Adding insult to grievous injury, many companies failed to mitigate cyber doom by not encrypting their devices, not implementing a data backup plan, or the mother of all blunders, not training their workforce on basic cyber hygiene. Worse still, hidden risks abound for the unwary. A devastating cyberattack is just moments away when C-suite leaders close their eyes to the hazards of shadow IT, data offshoring, mobile devices, and social media.

Mobilizing the C-Suite: Waging War Against Cyberattacks is a call to arms for C-suite leaders to implement the tried-and-true cybersecurity countermeasures proven to thwart cyberattacks. In addition, this book is a handy, entertaining guide instilling fundamental cybersecurity principles to non-geek C-suite leaders.

Though written for the C-suite, this book is valuable for any leader in any sector or industry. Frontline cybersecurity and privacy professionals will find this book an essential resource for workforce cybersecurity education and training. This is also the perfect book to introduce real-world cybersecurity and data privacy principles to undergraduate and graduate college students.

Cyberattacks are an existential threat to your business. However, by focusing on the basics of cybersecurity, C-suite leaders can thwart even the most sophisticated cybercriminals and fight back against destructive cyberattacks.

Keywords

cybersecurity awareness; teaching cybersecurity; cybersecurity for executives; cybersecurity for business; cybersecurity leadership; cyber warfare; C-suite

Contents

Preface

In the 2016 Presidential debate, candidate Donald J. Trump responded to candidate Hilary Clinton's claims about Russian hacking, "It could be Russia but it could be China, it could be lots of people. It could be somebody that sits on their bed that weighs 400 pounds." I want you to hear me loud and clear: you will not be hacked by a hoodie-wearing, bed-sitting adolescent pecking away on a laptop. Cyberattacks deployed against your company will be perpetrated by smart, cunning, and highly adept cybercriminals who are financially or politically motivated in taking your business down.

Terrorist groups and criminal organizations invest in talent like any other enterprise—they even offer hacking training programs and recruit candidates who have specific cyber skillsets. What else would you expect from cybercriminal gangs trolling the Dark Web with ransomware toolkits on sale for less than a C-note payable in bitcoin? Purveyors of ransomware-as-a-service (RaaS) need experienced software developers, and good talent is so hard to find these days....

It goes without saying no industry is safe from cyberattacks. Cybercriminals care not if you are a head-banging rock n' roller or a country music fan, a wealthy aristocrat or someone living on food stamps, a lifelong vegetarian, or a ravenous carnivore about to scarf down a Big Mac. Cybercriminals are hell-bent on stealing your personal data, business secrets, or shuttering your company's network with destructive malware until a ransom is paid.

Even worse, cybercriminals have no compunction about deploying cyberattacks to maim and kill in order to achieve religious or political goals. Guilty feelings? Nope. Cybercriminals have no qualms about launching devastating ransomware attacks to blackmail organizations for personal gain.

Companies worldwide are operating in a cyber minefield against threat actors with the financial and intellectual firepower to wipe out businesses and obliterate critical infrastructure to an extent that rivals conventional warfare. Simply put, cyberattacks are an existential threat to your business.

No one knows this better than Jamie Dimon, Chief Executive Officer (CEO) of the financial services giant JP Morgan, warning in his 2018 Letter to Shareholders, "The threat of cyber security may very well be the biggest threat to the U.S. financial system." But Mr. Dimon is not alone in his fears about cybersecurity. At a congressional hearing in 2021, the CEOs of Citigroup, Goldman Sachs, Morgan Stanley, and Wells Fargo warned cyberattacks are the greatest threat to their organizations and the financial system at large.

Even Federal Reserve Chair Jerome Powell has freak-out moments over cybersecurity. At the Semiannual Monetary Policy Report to Congress in July 2021, Senator Jon Ossof asked Mr. Powell what he believed were "the greatest systemic threats to financial stability in the U.S. or globally." Mr. Powell did not skip a beat, "I'd have to say that the thing that worries me the most is really cyber risk. We haven't had to face a significant cyber event from a financial stability standpoint, and I hope we don't, but that's the thing I worry the most about. We have a playbook for bad lending and bad risk management, and we have a lot of capital in the system. But, you know, cyber as you see with the ransomware issues now, it's just an ongoing race really to keep up."

Let that sink in a bit. COVID-19 is ravaging the planet, supply chains are broken, climate change threatens the world, the specter of recession is rising—and yet Mr. Powell's biggest worry is ransomware!

Mr. Powell is right to sleep with one eye open on cybersecurity, given that the ransomware epidemic continues unabated. C-suite leaders are likewise painfully aware of the countless cyberattacks raging across the planet wreaking havoc with massive data breaches and network shutdowns. It's no wonder C-suite leaders are bone-chilling, freaked-out terrified about the impact a vicious cyberattack could have on their company, employees, and customers.

A massive data breach or physically destructive cyberattack will result in a public relations disaster, not to mention lawsuits, fines and penalties, and the personal humiliation of company executives who failed to do enough to prevent a cyber catastrophe from happening. Fear is a perfectly rational state of being for C-suite leaders, who have the duty and privilege of safeguarding the organization's most precious of assets—terabytes of personal, financial, or health data whose loss would devastate the lives of their customers, colleagues, and the community writ large.

This book was written to help C-suite leaders navigate their organization through today's uncharted waters made more treacherous by a global pandemic and the tenaciousness of cybercriminals. However, this book is useful for all leaders of an organization—be they managers, directors, vice presidents, or board members—who seek practical steps to thwarting cybercriminals by building a cyber-resilient company. This book will provide leaders with awareness of cyber risks and cybersecurity best practices so they can fully discharge their managerial and fiduciary obligations to the organization.

To beat back the cybercriminals, companies must focus on the low-hanging fruits of cybersecurity. It's all about the basics. If you can't get the simple stuff right, nothing else will matter—not a billion-dollar budget, not thousands of cyber-deployed staff, not even bleeding edge countermeasures using machine learning and artificial intelligence will stop a devastating cyberattack.

Like COVID-19, ransomware is an epidemic blazing across the globe. Go ahead and google *ransomware cyberattacks* and you will find scores of world-class companies hacked nearly to the brink of death by network encrypting malware. Then, dig a little deeper, and you will find the root cause of ransomware hell is failing to implement basic *cyber hygiene.*

Scrubbing your teeth twice a day with fluoride toothpaste means less time in the dentist's chair. Rolling up your sleeve for a COVID-19 jab keeps you off a respirator. Just like personal hygiene keeps you in the pink of health, good cyber hygiene keeps your company healthy by inoculating your business against infection from malware-injecting cybercriminals.

Companies laid low by ransomware failed to practice good cyber hygiene by using weak or reused passwords, not turning on multifactor authentication, or neglecting to install patches to known software vulnerabilities. Adding fuel to the fire, many companies failed to mitigate cyber doom by not encrypting their devices, not implementing a data backup plan, or the mother of all blunders, not training their workforce on basic cyber hygiene.

Worse still, hidden risks abound for the unwary. A devastating cyber-attack is just moments away when C-suite leaders close their eyes to the hazards of shadow IT, data offshoring, mobile devices, and social media.

It's no surprise that C-suite leaders are being shown the door when a cyberattack strikes. And why shouldn't they be? Someone needs to be held accountable when a cyberattack results in a massive data breach or shuts down a network affecting millions of people. The good news is C-suite leaders can do plenty to protect their organizations by focusing on the simple stuff along the journey toward a mature cybersecurity program.

The goal of this book is to enlighten C-suite leaders on the cyberse-curity countermeasures a company should implement to defeat ransom-ware cyberattacks. To achieve this goal, the book highlights notorious cyberattacks to demonstrate how basic cyber hygiene can thwart even the most determined cybercriminals. In addition, chief information security officers (CISOs) and chief privacy officers (CPOs) can use this book as a handy, engaging guide to instill basic privacy and cybersecurity principles to non-techy C-suite leaders. Most importantly, the book is also an excel-lent resource for companywide cyber hygiene training.

Cyberattacks and data breaches are worse now than ever before. However, by focusing on the basics of cybersecurity, C-suite leaders can defeat even the most sophisticated cybercriminals and fight back against company-killing cyberattacks.

Acknowledgments

Writing a book is hard, but writing a book on cybersecurity and data privacy is like dismantling a Honda Accord and reassembling the humble sedan into a bad-boy Porsche Boxster. Nothing is more technically complex than cybersecurity or as legally byzantine as data privacy, but both are among the greatest existential risks to organizations worldwide.

On top of the tightly wound knottiness of the subject matter, I'll throw in that nobody knows it all, and that goes triple for your humble author. That's why in writing this book, I leaned heavily on two experts in cybersecurity and data privacy who tested my assumptions, bounced ideas around, and generally provided wisdom and guidance that helped me create the book now in your hands.

Matthew Schmidt is a cybersecurity consultant and blogger specializing in penetration testing and ethical hacking. He'll don a white hat, metaphorically speaking, to penetrate a company's network, even if it means climbing through a third-floor window, picking the lock on the door to the server room, or cracking a wireless network with a Wi-Fi Pineapple. If there's an exploitable vulnerability, better it is found by a white hat who'll tell you how to correct the problem than a cybercriminal eager to inject a ransomware payload.

Jennifer Young is the director of compliance and privacy for a large health system who possesses deep expertise in privacy, cybersecurity, and healthcare compliance. She's an executive leader who can build an effective compliance program from scratch and is one of the few people I know that love conflicts of interest (preventing them, that is!). Jennifer is a certified professional compliance officer and is certified in healthcare privacy compliance.

Special thanks to the teams at Business Expert Press and Exeter Premedia Services for their editing, marketing, and all-around publishing expertise.

CHAPTER 1

The One Reason Why Cyberattacks Are Worse Now Than Ever Before

Nothing is safe from a cyberattack, not even breakfast. Bagel fans in the United States broke out in a cold sweat when cream cheese vanished from bakeries and bagel shops at the close of 2021. COVID-19 supply chain bottlenecks played a role, but American bagelholics went into sudden withdrawal mostly because a cyberattack shuttered the dairy production of the largest cream cheese manufacturer in the United States.

It's no schmear campaign; cybercriminals caused the Great Cream Cheese Shortage of 2021. Shortly before Thanksgiving in the United States, ransomware infected the computer systems of dairy behemoth Schreiber Foods, a Wisconsin-based producer of cream cheese, milk, and yogurt, gumming up the company's plants and distribution centers nationwide.

Ransomware cyberattacks use malicious software, or malware, to encrypt a company's data until a ransom is paid. Food processing companies make mouthwatering targets for cybercriminals because the food and beverage supply chain is rife with hackable vulnerabilities; likewise, the public tends to notice when a beloved staple is missing from supermarket shelves.

Cybercriminals are tenacious hunters, and many other industries are locked in the crosshairs. The lure of scoring a hefty ransomware payment for switching the lights back on is incentive enough for cybercriminals to focus their sights on utility companies. Hospitals find themselves smack dab in the middle of a bullseye because shuttered health information systems must be restored to provide patient care.

In addition to locking out a company from its data, cybercriminals may *exfiltrate* (which sounds way cooler than steal) gigabytes of data and demand ransom in return for not publicly posting the data on the Dark Web. The *Dark Web* conjures a host of scary images, but really it is just the part of the Internet you can't reach with plain-vanilla browsers like Microsoft Edge or Google Chrome. The Dark Web is only accessible with *The Onion Router* browser, succinctly known as *Tor*, and is a place where criminals go to trade illegal drugs or stolen passwords.

No doubt about it, ransomware will make you break open the piggy bank, but perhaps worse than the hit to Schreiber Foods' wallet was the sight of bagel addicts going cold turkey, curling into a fetal position as cream cheese melted from store shelves. Nothing is sacred to cybercriminals, not even a poppy seed bagel with garlic and herb schmear.

But don't assume cybercriminals are merely lactose intolerant; apparently, they have a beef with jerky as well. The cream cheese smackdown came on the heels of a ransomware attack on Brazilian meatpacking giant JBS Foods, which paid an $11 million ransom in bitcoin as a cyberattack shut down the company's meat processing plants in the United States.

Ransomware became a household word in 2021, linking an epidemic of cyberattacks to an angst-ridden global zeitgeist spawned by the January 6 Insurrection, chaotic U.S. withdrawal from Afghanistan, and rise of the Delta variant. Phew, what a rotten year!

But nothing says ransomware like an empty gas tank. In May 2021, a ransomware attack brought down the largest gas pipeline in the United States, triggering fuel shortages along the East Coast for nearly a week. Colonial Pipeline, headquartered in Georgia, is a mammoth pipeline operator, delivering fuel to nearly half the East Coast along 5,500 miles of pipeline stretching from Texas to New Jersey. Colonial Pipeline's system was hacked by an Eastern European cybercriminal gang known as DarkSide. DarkSide slipped into the company's system via a virtual private network (VPN) used by company employees to work remotely. It is not known how, but DarkSide obtained an employees' username and password to log into the VPN. Once inside Colonial Pipeline's network, DarkSide stole 100 gigabytes of data before infecting the pipeline company's system with ransomware.

The ransomware primarily struck the company's billing systems; however, executives of the company shut down the pipeline as a precautionary measure to prevent the ransomware from spreading to the operational systems transporting fuel through the pipelines. Of preemptively shutting down the pipeline, CEO Joseph Blount said, "It was absolutely the right thing to do. At the time, we had no idea who was attacking us or what their motives were."

Colonial Pipeline paid a ransom of 75 bitcoins (worth about $4.4 million at the time) to obtain the decryption key from the cybercriminals to unlock the company's systems (the cybercriminals had also threatened to publicly release the 100 gigabytes of data they stole if the ransom was not paid). The ransomware attack also resulted in the company sending breach notification letters to about 6,000 individuals, mostly employees and family members, whose personal information had been compromised.

Ransomware in the Age of COVID-19

As ransomware infected computer systems across the globe, COVID-19 infected people's bodies. The spiky virus inflames the human respiratory tract causing fever, chills, difficulty in breathing, loss of taste or smell, nausea, diarrhea—and for millions of people, a gruesome death. Coming on the heels of the global pandemic, the cyberattacks on Schreiber Foods, JBS, and Colonial Pipeline made 2021 a banner year for cybercriminals. But as bad as the epidemic of ransomware was, at least it didn't kill anyone. But could it?

COVID-19 gutted the healthcare ecosystem and exposed the fragility of healthcare organizations worldwide. Would cybercriminals leverage the chaos of COVID-19 to launch cyberattacks on overwhelmed hospitals to injure vulnerable, critically ill patients? Could a cybercriminal hack into a diabetic patient's insulin pump and trick it into delivering a fatal overdose? Or infect a pacemaker with malware to produce high-voltage shocks lethal to the patient?

This is not the plot of a James Bond movie; the U.S. Food and Drug Administration (FDA) has warned cybersecurity vulnerabilities may allow a cybercriminal to seize control of medical devices connecting to wireless networks, such as medical imaging systems, anesthesia machines, and infusion pumps. Cybercriminals could remotely hijack a medical device to alter its purpose, cause a malfunction, or shut it down. Chillingly, a cybercriminal could remotely direct an insulin pump to halt the insulin dose, triggering life-threatening diabetic ketoacidosis.

The stakes are high, and cybercriminals know when to strike. Holidays and weekends are prime time for a cyberattack because businesses are closed and employees are on vacation. This has led the Federal Bureau of Investigation (FBI) and the Cybersecurity and Infrastructure Security Agency (CISA) to issue joint alerts around the holidays warning organizations to remain vigilant and protect themselves against cyberattacks. On cue, CISA Director Jen Easterly said in a statement released on the Monday before Thanksgiving, "We know that threat actors don't take holidays."

Armageddon Out of Here

An SUV running on empty due to a cyberattack is terribly inconvenient; a blueberry bagel sans a hefty dollop of schmear is, well, downright criminal. But a devastating cyberattack on critical infrastructure would bring evil to a whole new level. When will the Big One happen? What would a cyber Pearl Harbor even look like?

To put this in perspective, consider the brutality of conventional weapons—think armed drones slamming into a nuclear reactor or military aircraft dropping cluster bombs on a hospital. Cyberattacks have the potential to cause the same level of damage as conventional weapons, but are harder to trace, granting plausible deniability to the nation-state threat actor.

Cyberwarfare is not something happening in a Star Trek alternative universe. It is actually happening now.

- In 2015, cybercriminals knocked out Ukraine's power grid, plunging 230,000 people into darkness for six hours in sub-zero temperatures.
- In 2017, the destructive NotPetya malware crippled Ukrainian banks, utilities, and government ministries. While

Ukraine was the primary target, NotPetya was so contagious it went global, spreading to Europe, Russia, and the United States. The virulent malware infected the systems of many companies—WPP (a British advertising agency); Merck (a U.S. pharmaceutical company); Deutsche Bahn (a German railroad); and Danish shipping giant Maersk—to name but a few.

- In 2021, cybercriminals launched a ransomware attack on two coal plants that, if successful, would have plunged three million Australians into the dark. Not to be outdone as a prime target for cybercriminals, Taiwanese officials claim the island nation is hit with *five million attacks a day* and point the finger at China as the likely culprit.

Ukraine, Australia, and Taiwan may be in tough neighborhoods, but cyberwarfare can easily come to the shores of the United States. In 2021, a cyberattack on a Florida water treatment plant attempted to increase the level of sodium hydroxide (which is lye used to reduce water acidity) to poisonous levels. The attack was fortunately thwarted but could have been deadly if it succeeded. Critical infrastructure, such as water treatment plants, nuclear and electrical utilities, hospitals, and fuel pipelines, make tempting targets for nation-state threat actors hell-bent on bringing the United States to its knees.

Coming Together at the Seams

Cyberattacks on critical infrastructure like utilities, water treatment plants, and food processing companies are made possible by the convergence of information technology (IT) and operational technology (OT). IT encompasses all the things that store, manage, and send electronic data (e.g., the computers, peripherals, servers, and other devices comprising the standard office workstation). OT is the hardware or software controlling the devices that do something in the physical world—think fuel valves, water pumps, automated teller machines (ATMs), and industrial floor scrubbers (which are surface-cleaning robots programmed to put a sparkle on the filthiest warehouse floor … *I know, cool!*).

Before the convergence of IT and OT, cyberattacks were pretty much relegated to data breaches, as OT devices were *air-gapped*—that is, not connected to the Internet. As such, it was nigh-impossible for a cybercriminal to gain access to an OT device and make it do something nefarious.

As digital innovation evolved, OT devices became part of the *Internet of Things*, creating new attack vectors with which to pummel freshly mushrooming attack surfaces, much to the delight of cybercriminals everywhere. OT systems are now susceptible to malware that could be used to shut down services, destroy equipment, and generally spew mayhem across the globe.

It's no wonder with the onset of *IT/OT convergence* we have seen an epidemic of cyberattacks on critical infrastructure.

- The Colonial Pipeline cyberattack not only resulted in data theft, but gas pipelines were shut down for nearly a week.
- Ransomware attacks on Schreiber Foods and JBS led to food shortages, raising questions about the security of the nation's food and beverage supply chain.
- In a close call, an attempted cyberattack on a Florida water treatment plant could have poisoned drinking water with excessive levels of sodium hydroxide.
- Cybercriminals knocked out Ukraine's power grid, leaving hundreds of thousands of citizens without power in the dead of winter.

Not even air-gapped facilities are safe. Cybercriminals have been known to seed company property with universal serial bus (USB) drives infected by malware. An unsuspecting employee will find the USB drive—and to see what is on it—insert the USB drive into a computer port and deliver the malware directly into the company network.

The most famous example of a successful cyberattack on an air-gapped facility is the *Stuxnet Worm*. The computer systems at Iranian nuclear facilities were infected with malware from a workers' compromised USB drive. The Stuxnet Worm did its job by causing uranium-enriching centrifuges to spin at erratic speeds and break.

In a nutshell, IT and OT systems are converging, and the future suggests greater integration, not less. I certainly don't see IT and OT as separating, given the incredible advances in machine learning, artificial intelligence, and other bleeding-edge technologies coming down the pike.

So like it or not, critical infrastructure companies will need to pony up beaucoup dollars for cybersecurity (backed by prodigious amounts of cybersecurity sweat equity) to ensure OT systems cannot be hijacked by cybercriminals intent on causing physical damage or, worse, death and destruction on an epic scale.

The Ballad of IT and OT

Rudyard Kipling's *The Ballad of East and West* begins with the famous line, "East is east and west is west, and never the twain shall meet." Much like the opening hook from Rudyard Kipling's 1889 poem, when IT and OT systems were like oil and water, cyberattacks led to data breaches and nothing more. A ransomware cyberattack was simply not worth the effort when an OT system was not connected with an IT system, so cybercriminals pretty much focused on stealing data.

But now, IT/OT convergence is in full swing, and utilities, pipelines, and other critical infrastructure companies operate in peril that a cyberattack could lead to physical carnage and loss of life. Even if an organization is not a critical infrastructure company, its physical operations have likely become deeply enmeshed with digital technologies.

Cybercriminals now have a two-track strategy when a company's network is compromised: first, the cybercriminal will exfiltrate massive amounts of data; next, the cybercriminal will infect the network with ransomware to encrypt the system and divorce the company from its data.

The cybercriminal, therefore, has two ways to make money. The cybercriminal will threaten to publish the stolen data on the Dark Web unless a ransom is paid, and rubbing salt in the wound, the cybercriminal will also demand ransom in return for unlocking the encrypted data. To make matters worse, the cybercriminal actually has a third way to make money—despite promising not to publish the stolen data in return for the ransom payment, the cybercriminal does it anyway, selling the data on the Dark Web to other cybercriminals for a tidy profit.

The convergence of physical and digital technologies has upped the risk profile exponentially. A company victimized by a ransomware attack shutting down its network will likely be dealing with a data breach as well.

Enlightened C-suite leaders understand that cyberattacks have become worse than ever because IT/OT convergence makes ransomware a more compelling proposition for cybercriminals and nation-state threat actors. Simply put, when IT and OT is integrated, the bad guys can wreak more havoc, in less time, than ever before.

IT/OT convergence is inevitable, as is the fact cybercriminals will take full advantage to launch withering cyberattacks that impact the real, physical world—and not just cyberspace. Fortunately, there are powerful countermeasures to reduce the dangers of IT/OT convergence. Collectively known as *cyber hygiene,* these best practices can repel cybercriminals like garlic wards off vampires.

In subsequent chapters of this book, you'll learn how to drive a stake into the ghoulish plans of cybercriminals by using strong passwords, turning on multifactor authentication (MFA), and installing patches to known software vulnerabilities. You'll also learn to entomb your data with encryption, and bring your network back from the dead with the resuscitating alchemy of data backup. Most importantly, you'll reinforce these countermeasures by bathing your workforce in the cybercriminal-frying sunshine of a cyber hygiene awareness program.

These countermeasures are an ensemble cast—and just like Anne Rice's *Interview with the Vampire* would be a flimsy novella without Louis, Lestat, Claudia, and Armand—there is no cybersecurity unless you implement all the countermeasures together. Companies practicing good cyber hygiene will have the best chance of staving off the dangers of IT/OT convergence; for companies that don't, it's a matter of when, not if, their network is slaughtered by a monstrous cyberattack.

IT/OT convergence may be inevitable, but a cyberattack is not, if companies implement the tried-and-true countermeasures of an effective cybersecurity program. The challenge is daunting, but not insurmountable. With humble apologies to Rudyard Kipling, in the age of ransomware, *The Ballad of East and West* sorely needs a geeky update:

Oh, IT is IT, and OT is OT, and ever fated to meet,
Like Earth and Sky stand presently at Elon's SpaceX fleet.

Strong passwords prevail, when never reused, and patches rule all,
upon routine install.
Turn on MFA, and do so today, with all your devices, when phishing
entices.
If a laptop is stolen, all hope is not lost,
When encryption guards your data, no fingers are crossed.
If a fire erupts, and a server farm crashes,
Backups revive the data, risen from the ashes.
There's no secret, no puzzle, no mystery to unravel,
Only use VPN, whenever you travel.
When the C-suite steps up with tone at the top,
Black hats are thwarted, and cyberattacks stop.
When cyber hygiene is practiced, as experience teaches,
There's neither IT nor OT, nor Ransomware, nor Breaches!

CHAPTER 2

Score a Knockout With Multifactor Authentication

It's the cybersecurity equivalent of heavyweight boxing champion Mike Tyson's famous warning: "Everybody has a plan until they get punched in the mouth." In 2021, a cyberattack on Colonial Pipeline roiled the East Coast of the United States with fuel shortages for nearly a week because the company failed to implement basic cybersecurity controls. The smackdown of Colonial Pipeline is a cautionary tale of the importance of not allowing employees to reuse passwords and closing old, defunct virtual private network (VPN) accounts when employees leave the company.

The details of the cyberattack are a bit opaque, but cybercriminals somehow obtained the VPN password of an employee who no longer worked for Colonial Pipeline. The ex-employee reused the VPN password for at least one noncompany website, which likely suffered a breach and perhaps the reused password ended up for sale on the Dark Web. So it's possible the cybercriminals who attacked Colonial Pipeline purchased the reused VPN password from fellow travelers on the Dark Web.

But there is another factor to consider. The hacked VPN account was not protected by *multifactor authentication* (MFA), a powerful cybersecurity countermeasure that might have stopped the cybercriminals dead in their tracks. Let that sink in for a moment. MFA laced up and ready to go like Mike Tyson could've pummeled the cybercriminals into the boxing ring canvas, gobsmacked, and down for the count. MFA could've one-punched the cyberattack to the other side of next week, and a jaw-dropping haymaker could leave ransomware too wobbly to infect Colonial Pipeline's network.

With MFA in the ring, the gas pipeline likely would not have shut-tered for almost a week, and Colonial Pipeline would not have forked over $4.4 million in bitcoins to cybercriminals. If MFA had been enabled, Colonial Pipeline, and not the cybercriminals, would've raised the heavy-weight championship belt in victory. MFA is perhaps the only thing tougher than Iron Mike.

So what, exactly, is MFA? If you have a bank or brokerage account, you probably have MFA. To log into a typical bank account website, you enter your username and password, and a numeric code texted by the bank to your cellphone. Some banks also allow the use of an authenti-cator app, which you can install on a cellphone, to generate a one-time numeric security code. Popular authenticator apps include Symantec VIP and Google Authenticator.

MFA is also referred to as two-factor authentication but the raison d'etre is multiple factors are used as evidence to prove—or *authenticate*—that you are you (and not a cybercriminal trying to hack into your account). With MFA, your username and password are *something you know* and the numeric code texted to your cellphone (or generated by an authenticator app) is *something you have*. So now the bank's website has two pieces of evidence to prove you are exactly who you say you are—meaning you are really you and not a cybercriminal—and can be granted access to trade stocks, pay bills, or transfer money to an individual retire-ment account (IRA). Some banks even allow for a third factor, *something you are*, such as fingerprints or a voice scan, for an even more powerful layer of security.

The extra layer of security provided by MFA makes it exponentially harder for cybercriminals to win. Even if cybercriminals stole your user-name and password, it would be impossible for them to access your bank account unless they also stole your cellphone. And even if they stole your cellphone, they'd have to somehow know your personal identification number, or PIN, to unlock the cellphone—no easy task (you do have your cellphone locked with a PIN don't you? If not, stop reading this book and do it now!).

You can see how the Colonial Pipeline cyberattack would have been thwarted if MFA had been installed on the compromised VPN account. So that's all there is to it—just enable MFA and chill. What could possibly go wrong?

Hitting Below the Belt With SIM-Jacking

MFA is a vital piece of the cybersecurity puzzle, but it is not perfect, and devious cybercriminals can bypass MFA with trickery and pure old-fashioned bribery. *SIM-jacking* uses *social engineering*—that is, trickery—to hijack a victim's cellphone, giving the cybercriminal access to the victim's texted MFA codes. Cellphone carriers, such as Verizon and T-Mobile, encode the cellphone owner's personal information on what's known as a Subscriber Identity Module (SIM), which is a physical memory card. The SIM card serves as the link between the owner's cellphone and the cellphone carrier. If the owner buys a new cellphone, the owner must either transfer the physical SIM card, or the information on the SIM card, over to the new phone.

Cybercriminals will deploy social engineering techniques in an attempt to hoodwink the employees of Verizon and T-Mobile into transferring the victim's personal information to a SIM card in the cybercriminal's possession. The cybercriminal may do this by calling the cellphone carrier and, pretending to be the victim, asking for a replacement cellphone, or purchasing an upgrade. Or the cybercriminal might just drive on over to the cellphone store and impersonate the victim. This can be incredibly easy to do if the cybercriminal has obtained the victim's personal data from a prior breach, either from a recent cyberattack or purchased on the Dark Web.

Often, cybercriminals will dispense with trickery and resort to bribing cellular employees with bitcoin to transfer the victim's personal information to the cybercriminal's SIM card. Be it through trickery or bribery, once SIM-jacked, the victim's cellphone becomes little more than a shiny brick as all calls and text messages are sent directly to the cybercriminal's cellphone. MFA is effectively bypassed because the one-time numeric codes sent via text messages are now in the hands of the cybercriminal. Armed with the victim's username, password, and MFA codes, the cybercriminal will take over the victim's personal accounts—social media, e-mail, and even bank and brokerage accounts are wide open for plunder and ransom.

When trickery alone does not work, and bribery fails to entice honest employees, cybercriminals will augment their cyberattacks with technology. One way to do this is to create a fake website that looks like an employee's company login page.

Cybercriminals will use a domain name that is similar to a company's website, so company employees accidentally land on the fake site. Employees then log in with their company username, password, and MFA code. The fake website can't actually log the employees into the company's network, so cybercriminals set up the fake website to crash, and with a realistic-looking error message, take the employee to the genuine company website. Having successfully phished the employee hook, line, and sinker, the cybercriminals now have the credentials and MFA codes needed to hack into the company's network and inject ransomware into the system.

Despite the threat of SIM-jacking, MFA in the form of text messages is a truckload better than not having MFA at all. But for extra peace of mind, a better option is to use authenticator apps like Symantec VIP and Google Authenticator. Authenticator apps are not linked to a SIM card; instead, they generate a one-time numeric code while installed on the user's cell phone. As long as the cybercriminals don't have physical possession of the cell phone, they can't bypass MFA from an authenticator app. You should also check with your cellphone carrier about additional security, like automatically locking-down SIM transfers unless they are unlocked with a PIN code.

The bell is ringing, so get ready to go the distance and be on the lookout for low blows and sucker punches from dirty fighting cybercriminals. But don't throw in the towel! You don't need to be an underdog, pulling your punches and fighting above your weight class. Get in the ring, put up your dukes, and don't take it on the chin. You can be a champ like Iron Mike and clobber ransomware with MFA.

CHAPTER 3

Credential Stuffing With Reused Passwords—So Easy a Cybercriminal Could Do It

Happy birthday, Password! The password blew out 62 candles on a birthday cake in 2023, but don't expect it to retire anytime soon. The venerable password remains the most efficient way to authenticate a user's access to computer systems and will likely be so for another 62 years. And yet, passwords are easily compromised by cybercriminals using a combination of trickery and technology.

Like Willie Sutton robbing banks "Because that's where the money is," stolen passwords are the obvious, and easiest, path to a successful cyberattack. It's no wonder the vast majority of cyberattacks are focused on hacking passwords, with *weak passwords* being the Holy Grail of cybercriminals and the golden ticket needed to break into a company's network.

Weak passwords are simple keywords like *iloveyou* or *password123*. These passwords are easy to remember but also easily guessable by cybercriminals, and should never be used. This bears repeating. Weak passwords are flat-out dangerous and tantamount to a custom-made, personalized invitation to cybercriminals with the salutation, "I love ransomware, please hack me!"

Strong passwords are hard to guess and consist of a complex keyword with a combination of uppercase and lower case letters, numbers, punctuation, and special symbols of at least 15 characters in length (but the longer, the better). A strong password could be something random like, *J329ke%#iou2k3%2* or a long passphrase with or without spaces, such as *myfavorite2moviesareneverontv*.

Strong passwords are the bane of *brute force attacks*, in which cybercriminals try to guess different keystrokes and phrases, hoping to hit pay dirt with luck and a weak password. But sometimes cybercriminals don't need to guess; they just use a password that has already been compromised to see if it will work on a different account. These stolen passwords can be bought from other cybercriminals on the Dark Web, a virtual red-light district bustling with criminal activity. Cybercriminals will then use *automated login tools* to try out the stolen passwords across multiple accounts. This cyberattack is made possible because people tend to use the same passwords for many different accounts and websites.

I'll explain how this works. Let's say Practical Paul has so many different accounts he can't remember all the passwords. But, Practical Paul has a brilliant idea! He'll create one super-strong password and use it across the board; this way, he only needs to remember one password for everything.

So Practical Paul sharpens his pencil and creates the mother of all strong passwords—*Hre3892bc4ek#qio@248NIue-29fenku3!*—a 34-character behemoth that he uses for his Facebook and Twitter accounts, his Amazon Prime account, and his brokerage account with TD Ameritrade. Practical Paul, being a retired bank executive, also has a 401k with his former employer, Breach Financial Bancorp, and he uses the super-strong 34-character password for that account as well.

On the day before Christmas, the notorious cybergang, Dancing Hyena, hacks into Breach Financial Bancorp's network and exfiltrates a treasure trove of data, including the usernames and passwords of approximately 11,000 retirement accounts. Dancing Hyena assembles these credentials, and with the aid of a login automation tool, sprays the passwords across many different sites. Armed with a reused password, Dancing Hyena charges headlong into Practical Paul's Facebook and Twitter accounts, where they post *Breach Financial Bancorp Stinks!* and *Paul has been Pwned!* Dancing Hyena also drains Practical Paul's TD Ameritrade account and makes distasteful purchases on Amazon Prime.

Poor Ol' Practical Paul learned the hard way that *credential stuffing* (using stolen passwords from one account to see if they'll work on a different account) and *password spraying* (trying a password across many accounts) is a piece of cake when passwords are reused. Just like weak passwords, *reused passwords* pose a grave cyber threat and should never be used. Reused passwords are the Achilles heel of computer networks and are highly prized by cybercriminals ready to strike with a quiver of malware-laden arrows. Logging in with unique, strong passwords for each account blunts the risk that a single, stolen password becomes the network's downfall.

Reused Passwords: A Tasty Treat for Cybercriminals

Reused passwords are the glaze on a chocolate frosted donut for hungry cybercriminals. In 2015, cybercriminals launched a series of credential stuffing attacks to scarf down nearly 20,000 customer accounts from Dunkin' Donuts. Deploying automated login tools filled to the rim with reused passwords, cybercriminals broke into Dunkin' Donuts network to steal prepaid debit card information, brand-named as *DD Cards*. DD Cards is a rewards program where loyal customers can order piping-hot coffee and yummy treats at Dunkin' Donuts restaurants. Stolen DD cards could be used by the cybercriminals themselves (hey, who doesn't love a Bavarian Kreme-filled Donut!) or sold on the Dark Web for bitcoin.

In 2019, New York Attorney General Letitia James announced a lawsuit against Dunkin' Donuts for failing to notify customers about their hacked accounts. "Dunkin' failed to protect the security of its customers," Attorney General James said in a statement. "And instead of notifying the tens of thousands impacted by these cybersecurity breaches, Dunkin' sat idly by, putting customers at risk."

Make no bones about it, sitting idly by in the wake of a data breach is an eyebrow-raising accusation. At the very least, you'd expect Dunkin' would've conducted a thorough investigation to get to the bottom of the cyberattack—that's an obvious first step, right?

From the New York Attorney General's complaint:

In 2015, Dunkin's customer accounts were targeted in a series of online attacks. During this period, attackers made millions of automated attempts to access customer accounts. Tens of thousands of customer accounts were compromised. Tens of thousands of dollars on customers' stored value cards were stolen.

Dunkin' was aware of these attacks at least as early as May 2015. Indeed, for several months during the summer of 2015, Dunkin's app developer repeatedly alerted Dunkin' to attackers' ongoing attempts to log in to customer accounts. The vendor even provided Dunkin' with a list of 19,715 customer accounts that had been accessed by attackers over just a sample five-day period. Dunkin' itself identified dozens of other accounts that had been "taken over" by attackers.

Despite having promised customers that it would protect their personal information and company policies that required a thorough and deliberate investigation, Dunkin' failed to conduct an appropriate investigation into, and analysis of, the attacks to determine which customer accounts had been compromised, what customer information had been acquired, and whether customer funds had been stolen.

Serious allegations indeed from the New York Attorney General. But certainly, Dunkin' would've taken urgent action to mitigate any potential harm to their loyal customers—a few logical steps that come to mind would be notifying customers about the breach, resetting their passwords, and inactivating the stolen DD cards.

Here's more from the New York Attorney General's complaint:

Worse still, Dunkin' failed to take *any* action to protect many of the customers whose accounts it knew had been compromised. Among other failures, Dunkin' did not notify its customers of the breach, reset their account passwords to prevent further unauthorized access, or freeze the stored value cards registered with their accounts.

Even after more than four years, Dunkin' has yet to conduct an appropriate investigation into the reported attacks or take appropriate action to protect its customers.

Moreover, following the attacks in 2015, Dunkin' failed to implement appropriate safeguards to limit *future* brute force attacks through the mobile app. The attacks, and customer reports of compromised accounts, continued.

The italicized emphasis on *any* and *future* is not mine; that's how it's actually written in the complaint. In fact, the allegations in the complaint burst off the page like flames, illustrating the New York Attorney General's office is not a cadre of folks you want to tick off. Written like a fire and brimstone sermon, the incendiary complaint should be required reading in university business curriculums, so future C-suite leaders understand the consequences of lax cybersecurity.

If there's one term summing up the complaint, it would be the word *pwned*, which is hacker slang to describe an utterly humiliating defeat. Pwned is pronounced by combining a *p-sound* with the word *owned*, as in the sentence, "Dunkin' was pwned by cybercriminals in a credential stuffing attack." The New York Attorney General's complaint is the prosecutorial equivalent of an Alan Moore graphic novel, portraying a company strung up, gutted, and totally pwned by cybercriminals in 2015.

You'd think Dunkin' Donuts would never let this happen again, right? The New York Attorney General's complaint goes on:

> In late 2018, a vendor notified Dunkin' that customer accounts had again been attacked, and that the attacks had resulted in the unauthorized access of more than 300,000 customer accounts. Although Dunkin' contacted impacted customers, Dunkin' did not disclose to these customers that their accounts had been accessed without authorization. Instead, Dunkin' falsely conveyed that a third party had "attempted," but failed, to log in to the customers' accounts. And Dunkin' falsely conveyed to some customers that the third party's attempts to log in may have failed because Dunkin's vendor had blocked them.

Alright, now you know why cybercriminals never order cream-filled donuts. It's because they prefer donuts filled with credential stuffing. Bwa ha ha ha! (Spoiler alert—the donut puns get a *hole* lot worse from this point forward. You have been warned.)

According to the New York Attorney General's lawsuit, Dunkin' Donuts did not notify its customers about the 2015 breach, did not reset customer passwords to prevent further unauthorized access, and did not freeze the credit on stolen customer DD Cards. Going from bad to worse, Dunkin Donuts allegedly did not implement sufficient cybersecurity to prevent another attack—and like clockwork, a cyberattack occurred in 2018, impacting hundreds of thousands of accounts.

To be fair, Dunkin' Brands, the franchisor of Dunkin' Donuts restaurants, disputed the Attorney General's account of the cyberattack. In a statement e-mailed to news outlets, Dunkin' Brands fired back:

> There is absolutely no basis for these claims by the New York Attorney General's Office. For more than two years, we have fully cooperated with the AG's investigation into this matter, and we are shocked and disappointed that they chose to move ahead with this lawsuit given the lack of merit to their case.

Tough talk from the donut maker; but Dunkin' Brands never got its day in court, opting to settle the lawsuit instead. The settlement was announced by the New York Attorney General's Office in September 2020, one year to the month after the complaint was filed. Dunkin' Brands, without admitting any wrongdoing, agreed to:

- Pay $650,000 in fines and costs to the State of New York.
- Notify customers about the 2015 and 2018 data breaches.
- Reset customer passwords.
- Refund any fraudulent transactions occurring on customers' DD cards.
- Ensure a cybersecurity program with reasonable measures to protect customers against brute force and credential stuffing attacks.
- Conduct an investigation when there is a reasonable suspicion a security event has occurred.
- Take corrective action when customers have been impacted by a cyberattack, including resetting customer passwords, providing notice to affected customers, and refunding unauthorized transactions.

Attorney General James took a well-deserved victory lap, gloating in a statement sprinkled with donut puns, "For years, Dunkin' hid the truth and failed to protect the security of its customers, who were left paying the bill. It's time to make amends and finally fill the holes in Dunkin's' cybersecurity. Not only will customers be reimbursed for lost funds, but we are ensuring the company's dangerous brew of lax security and negligence comes to an end."

So it seems Dunkin' finally woke up and smelled the coffee! Yet early on in 2015, Dunkin' could have told its customers about the cyberattack, reset the compromised passwords, and refunded any unauthorized loyalty card transactions. Dunkin' also could have taken steps to guard against future brute force attacks. Multifactor authentication—MFA for short—could have been provided as an added layer of security, and monitoring software could have been installed to alert management about any surges in failed logins (which would indicate a credential stuffing attack is underway). Had these steps been taken in 2015, the 2018 cyberattack might never have happened.

Lower the Risk of a Cyberattack With the No-Reused Passwords Diet

A super-sized bottle of Nexium will not quell the acid reflux blistering your esophagus when cybercriminals lock your accounts with ransomware. Reused passwords are not part of a balanced diet and taste like sewage even when paired with a Dunkin' Hazelnut Mocha. But you can avoid indigestion—and cyberattacks—by using strong, unique passwords for each account login.

Remembering a gazillion different passwords is a feat of mental dexterity few possess, so it's smart to use a *password manager* such as *1Password, Dashlane,* or *Bitwarden* to do the heavy lifting for you. Password managers can create strong passwords for each account, so you don't have to worry about remembering them. Also, some password managers will alert you when a compromised password has been posted on the Dark Web.

However, a word of caution about password managers: It's important to do your homework when selecting a password manager because some are more secure than others. For example, 1Password has never experienced a data breach, while the popular *LastPass* has been hacked six times—2011, 2015, 2016, 2017, 2019, and 2022. Although the first five incidents were relatively minor, the sixth was truly a debacle. According to the breach notice issued by LastPass on December 22, 2022, a threat actor was able to copy a backup of customer vault data containing "unencrypted data, such as website URLs, as well as fully-encrypted sensitive fields such as website usernames and passwords, secure notes, and form-filled data."

First, it's disappointing the best LastPass could do was publish the breach notice a few days before Christmas, when people are on vacation and many LastPass business clients are closed for the holidays. Second, this is a potentially mind-blowing breach. LastPass customers use a master password to log into their LastPass account, so customers who used a weak password (e.g., password123) as their master password are in grave peril—cybercriminals deploying brute force techniques could guess the master password to access the encrypted data and the treasure trove of passwords therein.

The LastPass breach is a reminder that even with password managers, it's prudent to use MFA as a second layer of security for all your accounts. So even if cybercriminals nab the passwords stored in LastPass, for those accounts enabled with MFA, they'll be out of luck without the one-time numeric MFA code. But if you're one of the 33 million hapless LastPass customers, I offer my condolences—perhaps it's time to switch to another password manager that doesn't have a history of data breaches—such as 1Password—and reset the passwords for every account you stored in LastPass.

The LastPass breach is truly disheartening, but don't throw in the towel on password managers—if cloud-based password managers make you queasy, another option is to use an offline password manager such as *KeePass*, which stores your passwords in an encrypted file on your computer, and not in the cloud. Of course, if you've been impacted by the LastPass breach, it's wise to change your passwords, use MFA where available, and get yourself a better, more secure password manager. These steps may seem like a hassle, but they are prudent, and worth the peace of mind.

Cyberattacks are sadly a fact of life, and companies are particularly vulnerable where the attack vector is compromised employee passwords. The good news is organizations can implement effective countermeasures to repel brute force attacks.

First, hard-wire the use of strong passwords; no employee or customer should be allowed to log into the company's network with a weak password.

Second, MFA is a strong defense against brute force attacks such as credential stuffing and password spraying. Companies should view MFA as the cost of doing business on the information superhighway; there's simply no excuse for not enabling MFA for employees and customers. On the flip-side, cyber-savvy customers and employees should see MFA as a necessary tool to keep their accounts safe, not as a nettlesome inconvenience. As cyber hygiene goes mainstream, companies failing to implement MFA may find themselves losing customers (and staff) to their rivals. Indeed, one can only hope that companies will realize cyber hygiene is a marketplace differentiator, leaving companies that fail to implement basic countermeasures like MFA at a competitive disadvantage.

Third, companies can implement monitoring systems to detect credential stuffing attacks. These systems can look for weird login patterns, spikes in failed login attempts, and even flag the use of automated login tools.

So go ahead and treat yourself to a lip-smacking Chocolate Butternut Donut and a piping-hot Caramel Macchiato Coffee, but stay focused and committed to a no-reused password diet. The Dunkin' cyberattack is a stark reminder that sugar coating reused passwords and glazing over breaches are grounds for misery.

CHAPTER 4

Phishing Is a Cybercriminal's Favorite Pastime

Chomping at the bit to answer a salary survey from human resources? Want to make a charitable donation by clicking on the link in an e-mail from your CEO? What about downloading the PDF attached to your CFO's *eyes only* memo on competitive intelligence? Your inbox is deluged with e-mails from staff, key stakeholders, rank-and-file employees, vendors, and, quite likely, cybercriminals trying to scam you.

Phishing is a fake e-mail crafted by cybercriminals to look like it comes from a reputable source, such as the company's CEO or human resources department. But cybercriminals may also create fraudulent e-mails to masquerade as a trusted colleague, local business, or even a government agency like the Federal Bureau of Investigation (FBI). Phishing e-mails look like the real thing and are designed to trick the employee into clicking on a link or downloading a file, which delivers a malware payload into the company network.

In 2020, cybercriminals pulled off one of the most brazen phishing attacks of all time against Twitter, a social networking site known for bite-size posts by users who compose punchy *tweets* that are restricted to a 280 character limit. The cybercriminals pretended to be help desk staff from Twitter's IT department in order to trick Twitter employees into giving up their usernames, passwords, and multifactor authentication (MFA) codes.

While the usual method of attack in a phishing scam is via e-mails, Twitter said in a statement the cybercriminals actually called employees over the phone to scam them:

> The social engineering that occurred on July 15, 2020, targeted a small number of employees through a phone spear phishing attack. A successful attack required the attackers to obtain access

to both our internal network as well as specific employee credentials that granted them access to our internal support tools.

Phishing by calling employees on the phone is known as *vishing*, and while it can be an effective cyberattack, it is much harder to pull off than a run-of-the-mill phishing attack. In a typical phishing attack, a mass e-mail is sent to the entire workforce. There is no specific target; the cybercriminals rely on the law of large numbers to work in their favor, hoping at least a small percentage of employees will be tricked into giving up their credentials. After all, if a cybercriminal sends a phishing e-mail to 10,000 employees, only one employee needs to click on the malware-infected link and the cyberattack is successful.

With *spear phishing*, cybercriminals put in a ton of sweat equity in researching their targets to launch a compressed phishing attack against a specific person or group. For example, in a spear phishing attack, cybercriminals might only send phishing e-mails to personnel in the accounting department or the human resources department; or, cybercriminals might research an organization's C-suite executives and find a vulnerability leading to an attack on just one person, such as the CFO.

Cybercriminals are always on the hunt for vulnerabilities to exploit. Cybercriminals will scour the Internet, scrape social media, and dive into news articles in search of an angle to trick employees into divulging their credentials or clicking on a malicious link.

A newspaper clipping about a CEO's trip to Australia could spur cybercriminals to send a phishing e-mail to accounting department staff in which the CEO requests an emergency transfer of funds to close an important business deal. Or, cybercriminals can glean enough information from a company's own website to launch a phishing attack. Many companies have a newsroom page to issue press releases in response to important events. Publicly traded companies may have an investor relations page to apprise shareholders of upcoming meetings and distribute annual reports. It's also common for companies to post internal policies and procedures for ease of access by employees and business partners.

Openly published company information is generally a good thing. Publically available reports, policies, statistics, and news items support a culture of transparency and organizational integrity, while freely available financial data is the lifeblood of shareholder decision making. That's the Yang.

Here's the Yin: any information made public on a company website is a rich source of business intelligence handing cybercriminals an edge, making it a piece of cake to target a specific group of employees with a spear phishing attack. What this means is companies must be circumspect about what they post on the Internet as cybercriminals can weaponize even minute scraps of information for use in a phishing attack. Though boring to the point of tears, cybercriminals will gleefully pore over humdrum company procedures and manuals to discover an exploitable vulnerability.

Knowledge is power, and phishing attacks will succeed when cybercriminals are steeped in a company's operations and are able to identify vulnerabilities of targeted staff.

In Twitter's own words:

> This attack relied on a significant and concerted attempt to mislead certain employees and exploit human vulnerabilities to gain access to our internal systems. This was a striking reminder of how important each person on our team is in protecting our service.

Twitter has been tight-lipped on the specific details of how the phishing attack came about, ostensibly for security reasons. Perhaps, however, sheer mortification plays a role: the mastermind who hacked one of the most sophisticated technology companies on the planet was a teenager from Tampa, Florida. His accomplices were a 19-year-old from Bognor Regis (a town on the south coast of the United Kingdom) and a 22-year-old from Orlando, Florida.

Don't let their swaddling ages fool you. This motley crew of young 'uns breached Twitter's best defenses to hijack the accounts of celebrities and politicians, including Elon Musk, Jeff Bezos, Kim Kardashian, Kanye West, Joe Biden, and Barak Obama.

Once in control of the Twitter accounts, they issued fake tweets to promote a bitcoin scam. These fake tweets all followed the same basic script: a celebrity would ask followers to send bitcoin to a wallet address with a guarantee that the celebrity would double the amount and send it back. Usually, the fake tweet asked for $1,000, promising to send back $2,000 in a very short turnaround time.

For example, here's a fake tweet from President Barack Obama's account:

I am giving back to my community due to COVID-19! All Bitcoin sent to my address below will be sent back doubled. If you send $1,000, I will send back $2,000! Only doing this for the next 30 minutes! Enjoy.

The tweets would be comical, except for the fact people actually fell for them, netting the cybercriminals over $100,000 in bitcoin. The Twitter cyberattack was an in-your-face assault on one of the most cutting-edge social media platforms in the world. The public nature of the attack and, one would assume, utter chagrin of Twitter executives, could be a contributing factor in the company's reticence to provide details on how the attack rolled out. Nonetheless, a picture of the cyberattack has emerged, thanks to an investigation by the New York State Department of Financial Services (DFS), which issued a report in 2020, calling out Twitter's lax cybersecurity.

From the DFS report:

The Twitter Hack is a cautionary tale about the extraordinary damage that can be caused even by unsophisticated cybercriminals. The Cybercriminals' success was due in large part to weaknesses in Twitter's internal cybersecurity protocols.

The cybercriminal trio may have been unsophisticated, but they certainly did their homework in planning for the phishing attack. They studied publicly available information about the operations of Twitter to find a vulnerability, sussed out the duties and titles of employees to gain their trust, and with a lot of chutzpah, a dash of luck, and weak cybersecurity controls, used a common phishing technique to hack a social media platform that in 2019 swelled to 139 million total users with earnings of $3.4 billion in revenue.

While Twitter remains close-mouthed about the specifics, the DFS report provides crucial details of how the hack went down. Glitches with Twitter's virtual private network (VPN) had become more frequent with the company's transition to remote working. The cybercriminals, in the guise of help desk staff, called Twitter employees and convinced four of them to reset their passwords to fix a VPN issue. The employees were then directed to a fake Twitter VPN website and told to enter their login credentials, which would be seen by the cybercriminals. In real time, the cybercriminals then entered the employee's credentials into the authentic Twitter VPN site.

Once the cybercriminals logged into the real Twitter VPN, an MFA request was sent to the employee's cellphone, and the cybercriminals simply asked the employee to approve the request. Ripe for the picking, these four employees gave away their MFA, no questions asked!

And there you have it: locked and loaded with employee credentials and bypassing MFA through trickery, three young cybercriminals hijacked the Twitter accounts of celebrity users and tweeted fake messages to promote a Bitcoin scam.

Truly a debacle for Twitter; some takeaways:

- At the time of the cyberattack, Twitter did not have a chief information security officer (CISO). Big mistake. When a company does not have an executive-level CISO, it begs the question: Is cybersecurity truly supported by the higher-ups? Not having a CISO sends a powerful message that cybersecurity may not be valued in the company. Just as bad, not employing a CISO is synonymous with a rudderless cybersecurity program hobbled by feeble to nonexistent cybersecurity controls.
- Don't give up on MFA! Just be aware no defense is unhackable, and any countermeasure can be defeated by a sneaky social engineering scheme and gullible employees. That being said, one way to strengthen MFA is to provide employees with a *physical security key* instead of relying on an authenticator app on their cellphones. With an authenticator app, employees can be tricked into entering the one-time codes into a fake

website, which is exactly what happened in the Twitter attack. On the other hand, with a physical security key, the cyber-criminal would actually need physical access to the employee in order to pull off the phishing scheme. A physical security key can be plugged into a device's USB port to authenticate the user or it can be set up to work wirelessly when in prox-imity to a device. To sum up, the highest form of MFA is a physical security key, followed by an authenticator app on a cellphone, and the last choice (but better than no MFA!) is to send SMS texts to a cellphone.

- The *Super-user* concept of an IT Admin with rights to do everything in an account is a dangerous relic of days gone by. *Segregation of duties* is one of the most important controls in cybersecurity—an employee who needs access to remove a user's inappropriate tweet should not be able to reset a user's password or disable the user's MFA. Tasks should be sepa-rated based on an employee's job role and subject to sign-off by another person. A logging trail should be maintained that can be audited on a routine basis or as needed to investigate allegations of misconduct.

- Hands-down the most effective defense against phishing attacks is an eagle-eyed workforce trained to shoot them down on sight. Companies should teach employees the ins and outs of phishing attacks, how to spot a fake e-mail or phony call, and what to do when a scam is in their sights. When employ-ees understand the mechanics of a phishing attack, they won't be tricked into entering their credentials on a fake VPN portal or approving MFA because someone asked them to. Employ-ees with even a basic understanding of phishing will easily catch a fake e-mail and, instead of clicking on a link and uploading malware into the network, will forward the e-mail to the cybersecurity department for review. No question about it, a companywide phishing awareness campaign is the biggest bang for the buck in an effective cybersecurity program.

You, Too, Can Be a Cybercriminal!

An organization's biggest cybersecurity risk is a successful phishing attack. Let me count the reasons why phishing attacks are both dangerous and plentiful:

- It doesn't take a rocket scientist to learn how to trick someone. Common phishing scams are simple enough for even the most unsophisticated cybercriminals to learn.
- Phishing scams do not require expensive or hard-to-master technology. If you know how to send an e-mail or make a phone call, you too can be a cybercriminal!
- Gullible humans are easily tricked because, well, we're not machines, and are prone to cognitive bias, emotion, and just plain screwing up!
- The law of large numbers favors cybercriminals. All it takes is just one employee out of thousands to click the link in a phishing e-mail to inject ransomware into the company's network. Only one employee needs to be tricked into giving up their username and password, and it's game over. The odds are not in our favor!

In a nutshell, simple, low-cost phishing scams can be deployed on a massive scale to trick unwary human beings. A cyber-savvy workforce backed up by an enterprisewide phishing awareness program is your strongest line of defense against a catastrophic cyberattack.

CHAPTER 5

The One-Two Punch

Password Management + Multifactor Authentication

Beating up cybercriminals doesn't mean fighting dirty; it means fighting smart. Sure, a round-house kick to a cybercriminal's solar plexus might be satisfying, but the one-two punch of password management and multi-factor authentication (MFA) will send cybercriminals plummeting to the canvas as if smacked on the jaw with a titanium keyboard.

Password management and MFA are the left-hand jab and right-hand cross of cybersecurity. Used in combination, they'll send the bad guys reeling and lay the smackdown on a potentially ruinous cyberattack.

Left-Hand Jab: Soften Them Up With Password Management

On one side of the coin, the venerable password is a simple and secure way to authenticate a user, making it a key defense against a cyberattack; on the flip-side, cybercriminals know how easy it is to hack passwords, making passwords an irresistible target and the focus of most cyberattacks.

The good news is you don't need to be a cybersecurity genius steeped in the ins and outs of brute force attacks and the many flavors they come in (such as guessing passwords, credential stuffing, and password spraying). It's enough you appreciate the valuable piece of real estate the password is, and understand your business will be pummeled by a cyberattack if you don't circle the wagons around each and every password used to log into your company's network.

So make life easier for your employees by implementing an enterprise-level *password management policy,* and be sure to communicate basic password cyber hygiene to anyone with access to the company network, such as vendors and independent contractors.

A decent password policy contains the following best practices:

- Requires strong passwords containing at least 15 characters with a mix of uppercase and lowercase letters, numbers, and special characters. The longer and more complex, the better!
- Prohibit the reusing of passwords. This includes merely changing one letter, number, or symbol to create a new password—that doesn't count! It must be a completely new password, unrelated in any way to the previous password … so be sure to change it up!
- Don't allow passwords that are easily hackable by brute force attacks. This means not using passwords that are easy to guess, such as the infamous *password123* or using a chronological sequence of letters, numbers, or symbols like *abcd, 1234* or *!@#$.* This goes without saying but never, ever use passwords that contain personal information, such as a name or date of birth!
- Do not allow the sharing of passwords. When multiple people use the same password, it is impossible to determine who actually logged into the network when a cyberattack happens. Also, password sharing gives a cybercriminal more chances to steal the password and launch a cyberattack. Bottom line, password sharing messes up the investigation and recovery, obfuscates user accountability, and increases the probability of hacking success.

These four best practices give you the flavor of what needs to be in a password policy—of course, this is just a start, and your CISO should be tasked with creating a password policy meeting the guidelines promulgated by the National Institute of Standards and Technology (NIST).

Right-Hand Cross: Knock Them Out With MFA

Passwords, no matter how strong, are not enough to protect companies from a devastating cyberattack. Employees can be tricked into giving up their username and password by slick cybercriminals—as exemplified by the successful cyberattack on Twitter.

Think of the password as the drawbridge to a medieval castle. Inside the courtyard is a cache of gold and diamonds, the king's treasure that outside marauders are plotting to steal. If the drawbridge is down, the marauders can saunter over the moat into the courtyard and plunder the king's treasure. But the castle also has MFA in the form of a portcullis—a dense, black iron gate—and even if the marauders cross the drawbridge, they can't get into the courtyard without the keys to the gate.

MFA is the extra layer of defense that saves your bacon when passwords have failed you. Recall from Chapter 2 your password is *something you know* and MFA's numeric code is *something you have*—put 'em both together and you've got yourself two fine rootin' tootin' bunch of factors! So even if nasty cybercriminals steal your password or scrape it off the Dark Web, they can't get into the company network without the MFA code. MFA is a powerful deterrent to cybercriminals and super-strong protection against a devastating cyberattack.

Imagine barbarous pirates roaming the cyberspace in search of undefended ports to pillage and plunder. Armed with phishing and brute force attacks, the vile brigands trick victims into revealing their passwords, or pick the locks themselves by guessing weak passwords. But MFA is a mighty incantation, protecting kings and peasants alike, by conjuring a medieval portcullis to guard their hard-earned treasure. MFA vanquishes phishing and brute force attacks because even if the pirate has the password in hand, it is useless without the second factor, a one-time numerical code.

But there is another cyberattack that can be very effective. *Keylogging* is spyware a cybercriminal installs onto an employee's device to record every single keystroke the employee makes. Keylogging spyware can be delivered when an employee downloads software from the Internet that is not what it purports to be, such as fake installers for videogames, or fake versions of popular Android apps like Pluto TV or VLC MediaPlayer.

Once installed, the keylogging spyware acts as a monitoring system that records usernames, passwords, and any other information typed by the employee.

MFA can defeat a keylogging cyberattack because even if the password is recorded by the spyware, the cybercriminal does not have the MFA device that generates the second factor, a one-time numeric code. The MFA device sits outside the network and is usually the employee's cellphone or a company-issued key fob. So even if the cybercriminal installed the spyware on the company's network, the cyberattack is repelled because the cybercriminal does not have possession of the MFA device.

So MFA is pretty darn great, yes—but it is not foolproof and cybercriminals have developed many tricks and strategies to bypass MFA. In Chapter 2 we discussed SIM-jacking and fake company login portals as effective ways for cybercriminals to bypass MFA. Cybercriminals will always find novel and creative ways to bypass any cybersecurity control, even one as powerful as MFA. It is therefore critical to supplement MFA with a strong cybersecurity awareness and training program as another line of defense from a company-killing cyberattack.

Step Into the Ring With the One-Two Punch

The big takeaway from the plethora of malware infections bedeviling companies worldwide is cybercriminals are positively obsessed with stealing passwords to launch cyberattacks. To accomplish their nefarious goals, cybercriminals deploy brute force attacks to guess passwords, while phishing scams are launched to trick employees into revealing their username and password.

Cybercriminals win by focusing on the basics of hacking, so companies must fight back by focusing on the basics of cybersecurity. This means organizations should require strong passwords that are never reused and train employees to be aware of phishing scams. Organizations should also deploy MFA as an extra layer of security in case cybercriminals are successful at phishing or buying stolen passwords on the Dark Web.

The cybersecurity industry is advancing by leaps and bounds with tools and platforms that use artificial intelligence and machine learning to stay ahead of the bad guys. But even the most advanced cybersecurity technology will not stop a cyberattack if an employee gives up a password or MFA has not been turned on. Organizations willing to step in the ring and throw the one-two punch of password management and MFA will have the best chance of beating the stuffing out of cybercriminals and knocking them down for the count.

CHAPTER 6

Got Patch?

The humble, squiggly earthworm is our planet's unsung superhero. Burrowing deep beneath our feet, earthworms mix up the ground, allowing water and nutrients to replenish the soil. Earthworms are hungry little buggers, munching on tiny bits of dead plants, fungi, and even dead animal matter; did you know earthworm poop is a great fertilizer? Juicy earthworms are a delectable treat for birds and other animals, providing a rich source of protein, iron, and amino acids. Earthworms are even edible by humans, and the squirming little critters can be boiled, roasted, or deep-fried and added to soups and salads.

Ick. Well, earthworms do not have a place on my dinner plate—at least not yet!

In contrast to the small but mighty earthworm, crypto worms have no redeeming value and cause nothing but wanton destruction in their wake. A *crypto worm* is a malware virus spreading like wildfire into computers by self-replication to encrypt the infected computer's data—in other words, it makes baby worms all by itself and those baby worms squiggle their way into computers one after another to infect networks with ransomware.

The first and most infamous crypto worm is the *WannaCry* crypto worm, which, in May 2017, slithered its way into 300,000 computers across 150 countries in less than a week. Once infected with WannaCry, a nasty message would appear on the computer's monitor, greeting victims with a ransom demand of $300 in bitcoin to unlock the data. Further twisting the knife, the ransom demand threatened the destruction of the victim's data if payment was not received within three days.

The good news is WannaCry posed no threat to large corporations that backed up their data. The bad news is small companies without a data backup plan found themselves swimming in virtual crypto worm poop, with no choice but to pay the ransom. Even worse, the victim's payment of ransom did not equate with unlocking the data because WannaCry could not link a ransomware payment to a specific computer. In other words, WannaCry could encrypt the computer's data, but there was no way to unencrypt, which means WannaCry was more an act of vandalism than it was an actual ransomware cyberattack.

God created earthworms, but cybercriminals created WannaCry by stealing a hacking tool called *EternalBlue,* purportedly devised by the U.S. National Security Agency (NSA). EternalBlue exploited a vulnerability in computers using Microsoft's Windows operating system via a flaw in the Server Message Block (SMB) protocol. Pretty complicated stuff—hey, we're talking about the NSA here—but basically, Eternal-Blue deployed malicious code by exploiting a weak spot in the file sharing rules created by Microsoft. Another way of looking at it: The NSA used EternalBlue to inject spyware into the Windows operating system (or any computer using the SMB protocol) to conduct intelligence gathering operations.

EternalBlue ranked high as one of the most successful espionage tools in the NSA's bag of spying tricks ... before it was stolen by cybercriminals! But NSA did the right thing and alerted Microsoft about the theft, and in March 2017, Microsoft issued a software update to quash the SMB protocol vulnerability.

One month later, the cybercriminals brazenly posted the EternalBlue exploit to the Internet, making the tool publically available for use by cybercriminals everywhere. To make matters worse, the cybercriminals also created a crypto worm, and in May 2017, used EternalBlue to deploy WannaCry ransomware throughout the world.

Most cyberattacks work by cybercriminals tricking an employee into clicking on a link or opening an attachment that injects malware into the computer network. But WannaCry is more sinister than a phishing attack because the crypto worm tunnels into the computer through a Windows vulnerability and then installs itself on the computer without any human interaction at all. Once inside the computer, WannaCry encrypts certain types of data files, such as the victim's photos and videos.

The countermeasures to phishing attacks are multifactor authentication and a workforce cybersecurity awareness campaign. For cyberattacks exploiting a flaw in software or hardware, the primary countermeasure is installing a code that corrects the error and quashes the exploit. This is called a bug fix or software update but is most commonly known by cybersecurity professionals as a *patch.*

Microsoft issued a patch for the SMB protocol vulnerability two months before cybercriminals launched WannaCry in May 2017. The Microsoft patch corrected the vulnerability and eliminated any possibility EternalBlue could be used to launch malware cyberattacks. Yet despite widespread reporting of the EternalBlue exploit and months' long availability of a corrective patch, WannaCry exploded across the globe, infecting hundreds of thousands of computers with ransomware.

It's a no-brainer: the only patch that works is the one that's been installed—and yet, failure to patch is a common cause of successful ransomware attacks.

Makes you WannaCry, doesn't it?

Make Way for Zero-Day

Patching systems is a key internal control to prevent a cyberattack. But what if cybercriminals discover a vulnerability before the software vendor catches on? Cybercriminals search for undiscovered software vulnerabilities like miners digging for gold. Software flaws allow cybercriminals to write malicious code to pierce through (or piggyback on) software products and inject ransomware into a customer's network. A *zero-day vulnerability* is a weak spot in the software discovered by cybercriminals (or, hopefully, by white hat cybersecurity researchers, affectionately known as *Bug Hunters*) before the vendor has detected the flaw.

When a zero-day vulnerability is discovered by Bug Hunters, they will notify the vendor about the flaw so that a patch can be created to cure the vulnerability. But if the flaw is first discovered by cybercriminals, then the potential for a destructive cyberattack is off the charts.

In a *zero-day attack*, cybercriminals exploit a software vulnerability to infect a network with malware before the vendor is even aware a vulnerability exists. As the vendor doesn't know about the flaw in the software, no patch is developed to stop the exploit. As there is no patch to stop the exploit, companies have no defenses to repel the attack.

A zero-day vulnerability is asymptomatic like pancreatic cancer, which, by the time it is detected, has metastasized to an advanced stage such that the cancer patient's chance of survival is low. This makes zero-day cyberattacks a fearsome cybersecurity threat.

When cybercriminals get their hands on a zero-day vulnerability, they can launch the attack in a massive phishing campaign, hoping an employee will click on a link in the phishing e-mail and upload zero-day malware into the network. Or, cybercriminals can scatter a few USB drives onto the company parking lot, betting an employee will insert the USB drive into a computer and infect the network with zero-day malware.

Hacking the DNC With Spear Phishing and Zero-Day Malware

In 2016, cybercriminals targeted the Democratic National Committee (DNC) with a spear phishing campaign using no less than six zero-day vulnerabilities found in Windows, Adobe Flash, and Java. The cybercriminals used social media to identify high-level staffers at the DNC and sent them fake e-mails that looked like Google security notifications. The *spoofed* e-mails directed the user to reset their password by clicking on a link. When DNC employees clicked the link, keylogging malware deployed, allowing the cybercriminals to see what DNC employees were typing. The cybercriminals were also able to take screenshots of the employee's computer screens.

The zero-day malware, combined with spear phishing, enabled cybercriminals to steal the username and passwords of campaign staff for then-presidential candidate Hilary Clinton. The cybercriminals used the stolen credentials to break into DNC e-mail accounts and pilfer documents and e-mails pertaining to Hilary Clinton's campaign.

Among those phished was John Podesta, Hillary Clinton's campaign chairman, whose personal e-mails were sent by the cybercriminals to *WikiLeaks*, the controversial and self-proclaimed library of censored documents founded by Juliane Assange. Mr. Podesta's e-mails were trotted out by WikiLeaks for all the world to see, much to the chagrin of the DNC and Clinton campaign.

One casualty of the cyberattack was DNC Chairwoman Debbie Wasserman Shultz, who resigned after leaked e-mails appeared to show her making salacious comments about Ms. Clinton's Democratic primary rival, Senator Bernie Sanders of Vermont.

Going Nuclear With the Stuxnet Worm

Launched in 2009, the Stuxnet Worm is considered the world's first cyberweapon, because it is the first time malware was used to cause physical damage in the real world. Stuxnet malware exploited a zero-day vulnerability in Windows to target an Iranian nuclear facility, Natanz. No one knows who created Stuxnet, but it is widely believed to be a product created by the United States and Israel to hamstring Iran's nuclear weapon program.

The Natanz facility was air-gapped, meaning it was not connected to the Internet. Air-gapping is a nearly foolproof countermeasure to thwart cybercriminals; if the computer system is cut off from the Internet, there is no way for malware to flow into the network. The usual vectors of employees clicking a link in a phishing e-mail or on a spoofed website are foiled by an air-gapped computer system.

But the creators of the Stuxnet malware came up with an ingenious workaround. USB drives infected with Stuxnet somehow ended up inside the Natanz facility; I'm not sure how this was done, but it was certainly a stellar feat of espionage. Once inside the facility, someone connected the infected USB drive into the Natanz facility network.

Stuxnet was the first malware to cause physical havoc in the real world. Stuxnet triggered increases and decreases in the speed of uranium centrifuges at the Natanz facility, causing them to break. The speed changes were so slight, it appeared as if all systems were operating normally, and the Iranians never knew what hit them until it was too late.

Patching the Blues Away

Imagine putting together a jigsaw puzzle unaware someone purloined several pieces and modified them to break the puzzle when inserted into place. Think of *patch management* as a defensive process of constantly updating the puzzle with refurbished pieces, so when modified pieces are inserted, the puzzle doesn't break.

Patch management is a vital process that helps companies keep their computer systems well-oiled with the latest software updates and bug fixes—before cybercriminals are able to launch a zero-day attack. In fact, not installing patches is a key point of failure for companies rocked by ransomware.

But installing patches is not fool-proof. Zero-day vulnerabilities are especially pernicious because no one other than the cybercriminals know they exist; as the vendor is unaware of the flaw, there isn't a patch to block the zero-day exploit, and the cyberattack is likely to succeed.

So, it falls upon companies to implement the ultimate cybersecurity countermeasure: the classic and pristine, tried-and-true *phishing awareness training program*. Do not discount the awesome power of a cyber-savvy workforce in repelling phishing attacks! The spear phishing attack on the DNC would have been thwarted if DNC employees had been trained to identify phishing e-mails and warned to never click on suspicious links.

Air-gapping is another anti-hacking countermeasure right up there with patching and multifactor authentication. Yet, air-gapping is easily defeated when someone physically injects malware into the network.

Here again, a cybersecurity employee training program can save the day. Staff should be educated about the cybersecurity threats posed by USB drives and other removable media devices. Pointedly, staff should be warned never to connect an unknown USB drive to the network.

Cyber hygiene works hand in glove with an educated workforce: Log in with strong passwords, don't reuse passwords, turn on multifactor authentication, don't respond to suspicious e-mails or click on dubious links and never plug unknown USB drives into the network.

And, of course, install patches like your company's life depended on it!

CHAPTER 7

Welcome to Hackersville

"Breach Financial Bancorp Inc. is not commenting on the cyberattack and we have no comments on whether ransomware was paid," a company spokesperson said. "However, we do confirm, emphatically, that Breach Financial Bancorp strictly adhered to the state and federal laws relevant to the situation, as well as ransomware guidance from the FBI, CISA, and OFAC."

The cyberattack on Breach Financial Bancorp landed the day before Thanksgiving. The cybercriminals chose the holidays to launch their cyberattack because most of the company's employees were on vacation, which meant it likely the banking giants guard was down. Better still for the cybercriminals, they knew Breach Financial Bancorp was suffering a major staffing shortage due to COVID-19, so the company was especially vulnerable.

"Breach Financial Bancorp should be glad we hacked them," said the cybercriminal gang Dancing Hyena in their public announcement taking responsibility for the cyberattack. "Once they give us the money, we'll restore their system and provide a report of how we hacked their network so they can prevent this from ever happening again. Pay us and some good can come out of this!"

The first prong of the attack was a spear phishing campaign targeting four employees who worked in the company's corporate philanthropy department. Breach Financial Bancorp was the City of Hackersville's largest financial services institution and had pledged $4 million to assist the Hackersville community with responding to the COVID-19 pandemic.

For three months leading up to the attack, Dancing Hyena researched the operations of corporate philanthropy and surveilled the four employees to devise a social engineering attack. This was an easy task, as Breach Financial Bancorp posted department policies and procedures to the company website. Of particular interest was a tranche of job descriptions, replete with titles and duties, posted on the Human Resources page of the company website.

Gleaning the job descriptions, Dancing Hyena became intrigued by the role of corporate philanthropy at Breach Financial Bancorp. The cybercriminals learned a significant part of the job of philanthropy staff was to respond to internal employee satisfaction surveys used to match employees with a potential charitable interest.

This triggered Dancing Hyena to scour the company website for philanthropy policies, and voila! The Philanthropy Department posted all their policies on the company website, to the delight of the cybercriminals.

Reading through the policies, Dancing Hyena learned how the philanthropy department would reach out to Breach Financial Bancorp employees to request charitable donations of time or money. Digging further into the policies, Dancing Hyena discovered an enticing operational vulnerability: the charitable donation surveys were generated not from the philanthropy department, but from the Human Resources department; thus, the makings of a successful spear phishing attack were born.

On November 24, each of the four philanthropy staff found an e-mail marked *urgent* in their inbox. The e-mail came from the company's Executive Vice President and Chief Human Resources Officer, with a request to click on a link and answer a brief employee engagement survey.

Three of the employees were on vacation and did not open the e-mail. The newly hired philanthropy analyst, Phil, was working remotely over the holidays to build up his PAL time. Phil clicked the link and a box popped up requiring his username and password in order to access the survey. Phil provided his credentials and, in-between sips of cold coffee, answered the survey.

A heartbeat after he pressed send, Phil knew something was wrong. Smelling a pungent sweet-burning aroma, he dashed from his upstairs office to the kitchen, where he barely got the turkey out of the oven in time. Phil had saved Thanksgiving dinner.

The second prong of the cyberattack was aided by a two-year-ago breach and the Dark Web. In 2019, a hotel chain headquartered in the City of Hackersville, Chintzy Inn and Suites, was hacked resulting in a data breach impacting nearly 200,000 hotel guests. The data stolen included names, dates of birth, e-mail addresses, and the usernames and passwords that customers used to log into the Chintzy Good Journey customer rewards website.

The cybercriminals promised to destroy the data in return for a ransom of $14,000 in bitcoin. Chintzy Inn and Suites promptly paid the ransom; however, the cybercriminals did not do as promised and instead posted an advertisement on the Dark Web selling a downloadable file containing the data of 200,000 hotel guests for $1,500.

One of the hotel guests impacted by the 2019 data breach was Breach Financial Bancorp's newly hired CFO. The CFO found it difficult to remember passwords and had dozens of accounts—work, school, brokerage, you name it—so for convenience, used one password across the board, for all accounts.

Dancing Hyena, an avid consumer of the Dark Web offerings, paid for the stolen Chintzy guest data, which contained the username and password the CFO used for Chintzy's customer rewards program. Dancing Hyena entered the CFO's credentials into an old, inactive Breach Financial Bancorp account that was linked to the company's VPN system for working remotely. As multifactor authentication was not enabled, the stolen credentials that the CFO had reused for Breach Financial Bancorp granted instant access to the company's network.

The two-pronged cyberattack worked like a charm. Dancing Hyena's access to the Breach Financial Bancorp network went undiscovered for eight weeks before the ransomware began shutting down critical systems.

At first, the company executives were feisty and refused to pay Dancing Hyena's ransomware demand. But Dancing Hyena turned the screws quickly, warning in a ransom e-mail, "We are officially tripling the ransomware amount if not paid within two days," and "we will post all your customer data to our information site on the Dark Web."

Six hours after the last message, Dancing Hyena doubled down in another chilling e-mail:

> You need to consider what your shareholders will think when your stock price craters! Don't worry, we can give you the encryption key to unlock your systems, and no one ever has to know what happened. We are professionals and will keep this secret!

By the next morning, Breach Financial Bancorp leadership caved and agreed to pay a ransom amount of $8 million in bitcoin. Once the cybercriminals confirmed the bitcoin transaction, they sent a final, conciliatory e-mail:

> Thank you so much for working with us. To further help you enhance the security of your network, we will provide you with a detailed cybersecurity report containing tips and tools for protecting your files. We will also provide you with verification that we have permanently deleted all the data in our possession. We are also available for further consultation at your request.

Six months later, in testimony to the House of Representatives Committee on Oversight and Reform, Breach Financial Bancorp's CEO said:

> While we experienced some downtime during the cyberattack, most of our network was up and running in short order thanks to our excellent IT folks and state-of-the-art back-up systems. We only paid the ransom as a precautionary measure to alleviate any unanticipated consequences—you know, it was more like an insurance policy.

Following the congressional testimony, Breach Financial Bancorp issued a press release announcing the CEO's retirement.

No press release was issued for the scores of executives who were terminated in the aftermath of the cyberattack, or who left on their own accord before the ax was dropped.

No press release was issued when Breach Financial Bancorp launched a systemwide phishing awareness program for all employees.

No press release was issued when Breach Financial Bancorp implemented a password management system requiring strong passwords that cannot be reused.

No press release was issued when Breach Financial Bancorp identified and deactivated legacy accounts.

No press release was issued when Breach Financial Bancorp enabled multifactor authentication across the enterprise.

Today, someone in investor relations is hoping to get out a press release in response to Breach Financial Bancorp's nearly $300-million-dollar breach settlement with the Federal Trade Commission.

But it is Memorial Day weekend, and the department is short-staffed.

CHAPTER 8

Me and My Shadow IT

Most CEOs would be flabbergasted at the ubiquity of technology within the company running outside the purview of the information technology (IT) department. *Shadow IT* (sounds ominous, doesn't it?) is hardware or software that is being used by the organization without the approval or knowledge of the company's IT department.

Let that sink for a moment. Your company is running on IT your IT department can't manage, monitor, and may not even know about.

Shadow IT is widespread because so many applications are easily available to the workforce for little more than an e-mail address. Most applications are free to start with, but offer tiered services at varying price levels. Think Google Drive, Amazon Drive, and iCloud to name but a few. All of these applications are available for free and allow employees to access data on any device, anywhere, at any time. So if employees aren't happy with the company-approved storage solution, they can help themselves to an off-the-shelf application at the click of a button. But hardware is cheap too, and many organizations are drowning in unapproved laptops, smartphones, and servers.

Shadow IT is popular because it's a way employees can get around productivity issues or perceived bottlenecks—especially when they think the company-approved software stinks and they can easily and cheaply (for free in most cases!) get something better on their own.

A classic example of this mindset is when employees use personal e-mail to handle company business instead of the corporate e-mail account.

Or when employees use Dropbox as their cloud storage solution instead of the company-sanctioned Microsoft OneDrive.

Or when the company's approved videoconference tool is Cisco Webex, but some employees use Microsoft Teams, while others use Zoom.

Or instead of using Google Authenticator for multifactor authentication (MFA), employees choose an authenticator app that has not been approved by the company's IT department.

Or—well, you get the picture.

But there is another reason why shadow IT is the norm in every company—it is because the C-suite demands it, sometimes even over the objection of the chief information officer (CIO) and chief information security officer (CISO).

Let me give you an example of how this occurs:

Dr. Whiplash is an orthopedic surgeon at a large metropolitan hospital where hip and knee replacements contribute substantially to the bottom line. Dr. Whiplash is also a nationally recognized expert in a novel, less invasive implant technique, and the hospital markets this renown to raise funds for its clinical research program.

Dr. Whiplash travels extensively conducting seminars on implant techniques, and while away from the hospital, Dr. Whiplash needs to answer e-mails from colleagues and patients. But Dr. Whiplash finds it cumbersome to sign in to the hospital's VPN account to check e-mails. The hospital account requires a strong password and uses MFA in the form of a one-time numeric code generated by a fob.

To lessen the hassle, Dr. Whiplash configured the hospital e-mail account to automatically forward all e-mails to a personal e-mail account accessed by a weak password and without MFA. To make things easier to remember, Dr. Whiplash uses one password for all accounts—banking, e-mail, shopping, you name it—and the password is *Whiplash123*.

The hospital CISO gets wind of this and asks Dr. Whiplash to stop forwarding hospital e-mails to a personal e-mail account. The hospital e-mails often contain sensitive patient health information, like diagnoses or test results, and the CISO is worried about the potential for a data breach. In addition, while all hospital e-mails are protected by 256-bit encryption, Dr. Whiplash's personal e-mail account does not have the functionality to encrypt e-mails.

Dr. Whiplash has been forwarding hospital e-mails for years without an incident and believes the time saved by not logging in to the hospital's VPN is worth the risk. Therefore, Dr. Whiplash refuses the CISO's request.

As a result, the hospital CISO puts in a ticket to stop Dr. Whiplash's e-mails from being forwarded to a personal account. Furious, Dr. Whiplash complains to the hospital's CEO and demands to be allowed to forward e-mails to a personal account. Dr. Whiplash points out the need for tempering cybersecurity with productivity and hints that knee replacement admissions may drop off substantially if this bottleneck can't be removed.

The CEO is well aware that Dr. Whiplash is revered by the hospital's orthopedic residents as a near god-like figure, but to make matters politically hazardous, Dr. Whiplash is a close, personal friend and golfing partner of the chair of the board of trustees, who is also an orthopedic surgeon.

After a quick consultation with Finance, the CEO breaks out in a cold sweat over the hit to the financials if knee replacements start to trend down. The hospital is about to expand services to a part of town that is considered a *medical desert* where residents have historically had little access to healthcare.

"No Money," the CEO mumbles to the Finance team. "No Mission."

The CEO's knees buckle (pun intended!), and the order is given to the CISO to stand down and allow Dr. Whiplash's continued use of a personal e-mail account for hospital business.

The CISO points out the hospital IT department does not approve the use of outside, personal e-mails for hospital business, especially e-mail accounts that don't require the use of strong passwords, MFA, or encryption. In addition, the CISO explains that there is no way the IT department can manage or monitor someone's personal e-mail account.

However, after receiving a flaming e-mail from the CEO (containing a lot of caps!), the CISO relents and restores Dr. Whiplash's ability to forward hospital e-mails to a personal e-mail account.

Three months later, it is reported that Breach Financial Bancorp has been the victim of a major cyberattack compromising the passwords of nearly two million of the bank's customers. One of those customers is Dr. Whiplash, whose password ends up sold on the Dark Web for a mere $4.98 worth of bitcoin.

Since Dr. Whiplash reuses a single weak password for multiple accounts, a cybercriminal is able to hack into Dr. Whiplash's personal e-mail account and finds a treasure trove of e-mails containing Excel files on the orthopedic clinical research program. The Excel files contain data on 800 clinical research subjects, including name, address, date of birth, diagnosis, test results, social security number, and prescription history.

One year later, the fines and penalties paid by the hospital—not to mention the reputational damage—far outweigh the admissions for knee replacements, which are nonetheless trending up nicely even though Dr. Whiplash has left the building.

Let's take a deep breath here. There are no bad guys in this scenario. Dr. Whiplash is deeply committed to quality and patient care; the hospital CEO is passionate about expanding healthcare services to the poor and underserved and needs a healthy bottom line to make that happen, and the hospital CISO is rightly focused on preventing a data breach or ransomware attack.

Shadow IT is a vexing conundrum for C-suite leaders as the use of non-approved technology offers benefits and risks that are both compelling and concerning. Add to this the dynamic everyone's heart is in the right place—the manager desires increased productivity, while the CISO worries about cyber risk—and you have a recipe for a lot of head-butting!

But you wouldn't be in the C-suite if you weren't up to the task of dealing with flaring tempers, and C-suite leaders can navigate the shadow IT puzzle by understanding its benefits and risks to find a solution that balances operational needs with cyber risk.

Let's start with some of the benefits. Even though software and hardware are cheaply and easily available to employees, shadow IT would not be so prevalent if the benefits were not substantial.

When employees choose the technology they are comfortable with, they will be happier and more efficient. In fact, their productivity should go through the roof! On the other hand, when employees feel like they are stuck with clunky IT-approved solutions that don't measure up, they can be demoralized and their work will suffer.

Employee satisfaction and increased productivity are a big plus for shadow IT. But—and this is a crucial but—the cybersecurity risks of shadow IT are ginormous:

- If employees are using apps or devices the IT department doesn't know about, then cyberattacks and data breaches might not be discovered until it's too late. It's not good when ransomware is discovered only after the computer network begins freezing up!
- The IT department will not have backup protocols for apps and devices not within their span of control. So if data is lost (whether by accident or theft) on a shadow IT app or device, the data may not be recoverable.
- As the IT department has no control over shadow IT apps and devices, it is possible employees will use weak or reused passwords. Also of great concern, who is patching the devices when software/hardware vulnerabilities are discovered? It's not likely employees will be tech-savvy enough on their own to install patches to prevent vulnerability exploits.
- If a shadow IT app or device malfunctions, the IT department will not have the expertise or tools to fix the problem, leading to downtime and productivity bottlenecks.

With a risk profile like this, it's no wonder shadow IT is the bane of CIOs and CISOs. But shadow IT can also be a productivity killer. Operational inefficiencies and increased costs are magnified when multiple layers of technology are used by different clusters of employees within an organization.

Let's say one department uses Microsoft Teams for videoconferencing, while another department uses Cisco Webex and yet another department uses Zoom. What happens when the departments need to collaborate but don't know how to use the other's technology? Also, economies of scale are lost when using many different flavors of products.

Shadow IT brings with it a host of plusses and minuses, not to mention heated exchanges between IT and operational leaders. When C-suite leaders are caught in the middle, it is important to remember both sides are trying to do the right thing, and shadow IT is both a risk and an opportunity.

To balance these risks and opportunities, CIOs and CISOs typically implement a framework for managing shadow IT using the following methods.

- **Outreach to department leaders:** The CIO and CISO need to meet with department leaders to understand their needs, frustrations, and challenges. Management should be encouraged to give the CIO and CISO a heads up before any unapproved app or device is brought into the company environment. The CIO, CISO, and management can partner by reworking cumbersome processes and selecting IT solutions that are both secure and meet the needs of the organization.
- **Employee education:** Employees who are educated about cybersecurity will think twice about using shadow IT because they will understand the impact of ransomware and data breaches on the organization. A cyber-savvy workforce is a company's first and strongest line of defense against Shadow IT.
- **Streamlined and transparent approval process:** There should be an IT review process so that employees can request to use apps and devices they believe meet their needs. The vetting process should be thorough but timely—if it takes too long for IT to approve or deny a request, then some employees will become frustrated and use shadow IT anyway. Transparency is key, so a comprehensive list of approved versus banned technology should be published so that employees will know what apps and devices they are allowed to use.
- **Scanning and threat assessments:** Audits, risk assessments, and scanning technology should be used to identify when and where unapproved devices are operating within the organization. Routine monitoring will allow the IT department to take action on unacceptably risky shadow IT, or initiate a discussion with leaders to correct significant but addressable cybersecurity risks.
- **Shadow IT policy:** An enterprisewide shadow IT policy that is communicated to the workforce will help employees get the apps and hardware they need to do their jobs while enabling

the IT department to tamp down the cybersecurity risks of shadow IT.

A framework to manage shadow IT will go a long way toward getting IT and operational leaders on the same page, up-front, to work out the security kinks and workflow hiccups that come with off-the-shelf apps and devices.

So ask your CISO if a shadow IT management framework has been implemented. If it has, then the vast majority of shadow IT challenges will get handled long before they become a C-suite-level problem. And this, C-suite leaders, is how you avoid the fearsome and cringe-worthy shadow IT showdown!

CHAPTER 9

You Versus USB

If you spied a thumb drive glistening with morning dew on the sun-drenched tarmac of your company's parking lot, would you pick it up, buff it to a clean, crisp shine, and gently insert it into your computer's universal serial bus (USB) port? Many people would do just that. Some out of curiosity to see what's on the thumb drive; others sneaking an altruistic peek so that they can return the drive to its rightful owner.

Removable storage media are small, portable devices that can be connected to a computer or network, such as USB drives, CDs, and external hard drives. Universal serial bus drives, also known as USB drives or sticks, thumb drives, and flash drives—are rock-bottom cheap and super convenient for storing and transporting massive volumes of data. But USB drives and other portable devices can be loaded with malware to exfiltrate data from the company network or encrypt the network to pave the way for a ransom demand.

Of course, it may not be about stealing data or demanding ransom. The motive for a cyberattack could be to damage critical infrastructure by a nation-state threat actor, or a gang of cyberpunks wreaking havoc for the pure joy of vandalism. A *USB Killer* is a USB drive that absorbs power from the device it's connected to, which it then discharges in a painful zap to fry the innards of the host device.

You can see why USB drives and other removable storage media are a tremendous cybersecurity risk for employees working onsite. However, the risks of malware-infused USBs are no less severe for employees who work remote. Indeed, the pandemic-inspired shift to working from home led to the unintended consequence of employees' personal lives becoming enmeshed with their remote-work environment. Cybercriminals have caught on and are eager to exploit this vulnerability with a new trick up their sleeves. Check out this letter from Breach Financial Bancorp, mailed to the home address of every employee in your company:

April 18, 2023

Dear Loyal Customer,

Thank you for being a Prime Rewards member! Your loyalty as a Breach Financial Bancorp customer means the world to us! To express our thanks, we are offering you a gift card in the amount of $25. You can order the free Prime Rewards $25 gift card by following the instructions on the enclosed USB drive. We appreciate our loyal customers!

Very truly yours,

Dan C. Hyena

Vice President, Customer Care and Loyalty

Imagine if this letter was sent to a workforce of hundreds, or even thousands of employees who are working from home? Perhaps office-based employees might be suspicious of USB drives sprinkled in the company parking lot. But would employees working from home realize the Breach Financial Bancorp letter is not a loyalty rewards program, but a cleverly disguised cyberattack?

If the company's work-from-home personnel number in the tens of thousands, as some mega-corps do, what is the chance at least one employee will insert the malware-laden USB drive into their work computer to obtain the $25 gift card? Cybercriminals love the law of large numbers! They know all it takes is just one employee to insert a compromised USB drive into a computer port to inject ransomware into the company's network.

Now, you may think your workforce is too savvy to fall prey to a hack like this. Well, think again, as cybercriminals have another trick up their sleeves for the unwary.

Road Warriors, an apt nom de plume for mile-hopping employees, often work during airport layovers or while settled in at a hotel lobby or coffee shop. Road Warriors are a stalwart band of professionals whose devices run down long before they do. A cup of coffee and a protein bar is all Road Warriors need to recharge their batteries; cellphones and computers, on the other hand, need electricity.

Thank goodness for all those conveniently located public USB charging ports! Found, well, just about everywhere, these little ports are eager to zap a parched cellphone's power bar back to a thirst-quenching 100 percent.

Here's the thing, though: those innocent-looking public USB ports may be stuffed with malware that will steal the data on the device it's charging, or infect the device with a nasty ransomware payload. In a *Juice Jacking* attack, cybercriminals take over a public USB port to steal data or inject ransomware as people are charging their cellphone or computer. So if cybercriminals can't get your employees to insert a malware-laden USB drive into their work computer, they will go the opposite route and trick unsuspecting employees into connecting their device to a corrupted USB port.

One last warning for the Road Warrior: If you're stuck at an airport layover and stumble upon a cellphone charging cord spread-eagle on a chair, don't assume it was lost and claim it as your own. The cellphone charging cord may be salted with a malware chip ready to inject ransomware when you plug your cellphone in for a charge. That's right, a lazy but clever cybercriminal may decide it's not worth the hassle to hijack a USB port, and will simply throw around a few compromised charging cords laden with malware to steal the data on your device or lock it down for a ransomware demand.

The point is, *any unfamiliar technology is to be avoided like the plague.* Never plug anything into your computer you did not purchase yourself, or was not given to you by your company. Likewise, public USB ports should be viewed with suspicion; better to just use your cellphone's charging cable and a standard wall outlet.

By now you can see the benefits of removable media—super cheap and super convenient—also work to the cybercriminal's advantage. Compromised USB drives and hijacked USB ports are a low-cost way to deliver byte-crushing malware into the organization's network.

USB attacks are as cheap and easy as phishing attacks. That's why they're so dangerous. So let's run through the downsides of removable media.

- Like a phishing scam, USB attacks are a low-cost cyberattack that can leverage the law of large numbers: It only takes one gullible employee for a USB attack to succeed.

- Removable media hold gobs (a technical term) of data. So if a USB drive is lost, the concomitant data breach is massive. On the other hand, a disgruntled employee can download gobs (there's that technical term again!) of data onto a USB drive and sell it to the highest bidder, such as a rival company or a gang of cybercriminals. Imagine the number of banker-boxes the cargo bed of a pickup truck could carry—well, a USB drive can lug as much or more, so if it's lost or stolen, the data breach is gobsmackingly (that's the last technical term, I promise!) large.
- Removable media is portable because the device is small. USB drives are easy to lose and darned hard to find when lost. They are also easy to steal and readily concealed in a sleeve or pocket. Just think of USB drives as "Data exfiltration made easy!" It's unlikely the removable device manufacturers will use that as a slogan, but it sure sounds like a rallying cry for cybercriminals.
- Road Warriors need a charge, and USB ports hijacked by cybercriminals stand ready to augment the device's replenishment with a painful injection of ransomware.

Malware-embedded USB drives and public USB ports are a cheap and easy way for cybercriminals to inflict withering cyber pain on a network or device. Fortunately, rock-solid countermeasures to reduce the threat posed by USB attacks can be implemented as part of an effective cybersecurity program.

A Barbaric Relic

My first recommendation is to implement a companywide *Device Control Policy* (DCP) to manage the use of removable storage media across the enterprise. The easiest way to implement a DCP is with *device control software* (also known as *USB lockdown software*), which will help identify all the devices currently enabled to connect with removable media. Armed with an inventory of USB-enabled devices, the organization can *whitelist* those business critical devices it wants to be USB-enabled, while blocking USB ports on others. The organization is now empowered to implement DCPs across the enterprise to mitigate data loss and theft. For example, blocking USB ports on non-critical devices means USB drives cannot be used to download data from those devices, and file transfer protocols can be enforced on whitelisted devices to limit the amount of data that can be saved to a USB drive.

While USB drives are a convenient method to transfer data, there is simply no technological reason why all employees in an organization must have them. With the advent of cloud technology, prodigious amounts of data can be stored on shared drives that are accessible 24-hours-a-day by employees and teams. So most employees can easily get their work done with internal file sharing systems.

By limiting the use of removable media, disgruntled employees won't be able to easily steal gigabytes of company data with a USB drive. Sure, if a disgruntled employee is bound and determined to steal data, they will find a way to do it, but data theft is a piece of cake with a USB drive, so why make it easy? USB drives are small and portable and easily lost or stolen. Limiting their use in favor of cloud storage will mitigate this risk.

Change is difficult, and most employees want the convenience and portability of removable media, especially USB drives. But these concerns are alleviated with cloud-based shared drives. The cloud is convenient and data can be shared between employees and teams 24/7/365.

Now, if an employee can demonstrate an unequivocal business need for a USB drive that outweighs the substantial cybersecurity risks, then perhaps the cybersecurity department can approve its use on an exceptional and occasional basis. But c'mon, does your entire workforce really need USB drives?

The economist John Maynard Keynes famously referred to the gold standard as a barbaric relic not worthy of a place in modern finance; likewise, the availability of cloud storage and device control software means USB drives are antiquated, dangerous pieces of technology.

Lock'em down!

A Software Solution

In conjunction with an enterprisewide DCP, organizations should make sure that USB drives are automatically scanned with antivirus software when it is connected to a whitelisted device. The antivirus program *might* be able to flag a USB attack when the USB drive connects with the computer. Unfortunately, cyberattacks using malware-laden USB drives—known as *BadUSB*—are notoriously difficult for antivirus programs to detect; so while it's still a best practice to scan removable storage devices, the better bet remains to limit their use pursuant to an enterprisewide DCP backed up by device control software. On top of this, be sure to install software that will automatically encrypt the USB drive when it's connected to a device. If the USB drive is lost or stolen, encryption should keep the data from falling into the hands of greedy cybercriminals.

When in Doubt, Talk It Out

Launch a companywide cybersecurity awareness program for all employees to warn them about the dangers of removable devices. Employees should be warned to never plug in any kind of unknown technology into their work computer—unfamiliar technology is *off-limits!* Training should warn employees about specific dangers such as a USB drive found in the parking lot or a discarded cellphone charger laying on a chair in the airport.

Employees should be cautioned to never charge their devices in a public USB port. Employees should use their own purchased (or company-provided) charging cord plugged into a standard wall outlet to charge their devices.

Personal and work life should be kept separate. Do not save personal information to company-owned computers or USB drives; likewise, company information should never be saved to an employee's personal computer or personal USB drive.

Removable media is cheap, convenient, and beloved by a workforce on the go. But it is risky technology prone to loss, theft, and malicious use by cybercriminals. The way I see it, we've got the cloud and shared drives that are always on and readily available, and we've got device control software that can help enforce a companywide DCP to limit the use of USB drives. So like gold doubloons, the $2 bill, and parachute pants, USB drives are a starry-eyed relic of the past that should be relegated to the dustbin of history.

CHAPTER 10

Data Offshoring

Out of Sight, Out of Mind

Offshoring is perhaps the most underappreciated risk in cybersecurity. There isn't anything inherently wrong with offshoring; on the contrary, the upsides to offshoring are so appealing, the practice is positively ubiquitous. But offshoring jobs or wholesale functions often bring data in tow, which ratchets up the cyber risk considerably.

Outsourcing an entire department—say accounting or human resources—to a vendor with staff located in another country is a common strategy to reduce costs and improve operational efficiencies. Sometimes, companies cannot fill high-demand positions in their home country, so hiring offshore staff is a way to manage the scarcity of talent. Offshoring also makes sense if a company needs 24/7/365 support, and geography and time zones are a barrier to servicing the needs of customers. Offshoring can also help with supply chain management, particularly when the supply chain in the home country is under stress.

Most people think that *data offshoring* means the data is physically moved, copied, or otherwise transmitted to another country. For example, a rural hospital in the United States, stretched paper-thin with a shortage of on-call radiologists, turns to a teleradiology company located in Mexico. The hospital transmits X-rays and ultrasounds to the company, and a Mexico-based teleradiologist interprets the images and sends a report to the treating physician.

Sure, that's one way to do it. But the more efficient way is to give the Mexican teleradiologist access to the hospital's *electronic health record* (EHR). The teleradiologist simply logs into the EHR to read the images and provide the interpretation. In this case, no data has physically left the

United States, but we still have data offshoring, because someone outside the United States can see the data. So it doesn't matter where the data actually is; as long as someone outside your country has their eyeballs on it, that's data offshoring. And with those offshoring eyeballs comes a host of cybersecurity risks.

First up, do most companies even know they're offshoring data? In the United States, it's the norm to contract with vendors for outsourced services in which data is seen and used. It's also possible the vendor could be using employees or subcontractors outside the United States who can access the data. However, there's no federal law requiring a vendor to notify its customers that they're offshoring data—so unless a vendor speaks up, a company might not even know its data is being seen and used outside the country.

This is a big problem, because if data offshoring is happening in the shadows, then cyber risks are not being managed. It's also going to be one heck of a surprise when a massive data breach explodes on the other side of the world. How does the CISO explain that to the board? Or worse, how does the CEO explain that to the *Wall Street Journal*?

It's hard enough to investigate data breaches within the home-country company; it's an order of magnitude worse when breaches flare up at an offshore location. Say a company's cybersecurity team is located in Los Angeles, but a cyberattack happens at an offshore location in Denmark. Has it been decided, in advance, who will lead the investigation? Does the cybersecurity team have the bandwidth to investigate a breach in another country? If not, does the offshore vendor have a solid team of cybersecurity experts that the Los Angeles team can rely on?

Complying with the privacy laws of multiple countries is another complexity. In Denmark, personal data is regulated by the *General Data Protection Regulation* (GDPR) as well as Denmark's law implementing GDPR. Meanwhile, back in Los Angeles, the CISO is fretting over California law, which requires notice to affected individuals immediately upon discovery of the breach. This begs the question, which privacy laws apply, and who will manage the investigation and breach notification to ensure regulatory compliance.

Protecting data is not easy. Breaches will happen even to companies with a team of cybersecurity professionals working onsite and around the clock. Imagine how difficult it will be to safeguard data that is located in a foreign country or accessible by people in different parts of the world. Monitoring network access to prevent lost or stolen data is all the more challenging across continents. And if you're not careful, the offshore vendor will have a Swiss cheese cybersecurity program—chockfull of gaping holes and easy pickings for a hungry cybercriminal.

In addition to poor cyber hygiene, some offshore vendors may be one bad day away from the poorhouse. Outsourcing to new companies and start-ups that are not well capitalized is a concern. Vendors operating on a shoestring budget may not have the wherewithal to set up a functional cybersecurity program. On top of that, a barely profitable vendor will not have the money to pay fines for data breaches or penalties for noncompliance with country-specific privacy laws. This leaves the company holding the bag when an offshore vendor drops the ball, and opens a slimy can of worms: who will the government prosecute in a big breach, the company or the offshore vendor?

In the United States, the *Health Insurance Portability and Accountability Act* (HIPAA) (pronounced Hip-uh, not Hippo!) is a healthcare privacy law enforced by a federal agency, the U.S. Department of Health and Human Services Office for Civil Rights, known by the acronym *OCR* for short. Now, let's revisit our rural hospital that overcame a staffing crunch by outsourcing medical image readings to a teleradiology company in Mexico. Let's say the teleradiology company is hacked by cybercriminals who exfiltrate a data file containing the health information of 4,000 patients. The information stolen includes the patient's name, date of birth, medical record number, and diagnosis.

The cybercriminals demand a ransom of $40,000 in bitcoins, or they will post patient data to the Dark Web. The problem is the teleradiology company is a six-person start-up with zero money to pay the ransom; so, gripped with sheer panic, the rural hospital steps in and pays the ransom. However, true to form, the cybercriminals cheerfully pocket the ransom but post the data to the Dark Web anyway, offering a cache of patient credentials for the reasonable price of $600 in bitcoin.

In a breach like this, who is the OCR going after? Probably not the offshore vendor, when there's a *covered entity* right here in the good ol' USA available for thrashing. So you can expect that the company located in the home country, especially if it has deeper pockets than the offshore vendor, is going to be on the hook for cyberattacks and data breaches that originate in a foreign country.

If that doesn't sound fair to you, try having an unemotional discussion with your customers when they find out their social security numbers were stolen in a foreign country. Put yourself in their shoes—when you go to a hospital, bank, or car dealership, your relationship is with that organization, not some business in Hyderabad (or the reverse, imagine how folks in Hyderabad would feel if their data was compromised by staff outsourced to Little Rock?).

Companies aspire to outsource their operations in a manner that by design is seamless and invisible to their customers. So when a breach occurs and customers are surprised to learn their data is being used by individuals in a foreign country, they naturally freak out.

Data breaches in a foreign country are bad optics. Breaches involving offshore vendors will make for a big news day and generate a ton of media scrutiny. If you have a public relations department, tell them to bring their A-game.

A Handy, Step-by-Step Guide to Offshoring the Risks Away!

Companies have a plethora of challenges in the age of COVID-19. Supply chain breakdowns. Inflationary pressures. A shortage of talent. The ups and downs of work-from-home technology. It's no wonder offshoring is happening everywhere. If anything, the trend is likely to accelerate as companies find their footing amid sweeping globalization and breathtaking technological advancement.

In fact, it's difficult for companies to avoid offshoring even if they wanted to, as more and more vendors have staff onsite at facilities throughout the world. Back in the day, a company could put out a request for a proposal (RFP), and if five vendors responded, maybe only two would be offshoring. So you could easily drop the two that were offshoring and offer the contract to one of the three domiciled in your home country.

Fast forward to the present day. You get a response to the RFP from those same five vendors, but now they're *all* offshoring. So offshoring has become very hard to avoid. Either you'll have to offshore or be left in the dust by your competition, or you'll offshore because it's being done by all your vendors anyway.

A wholesale ban on offshoring will likely not be feasible, so companies are left with two options: offshore data until the cows come home or develop an offshoring risk management program to avoid a destructive cyberattack or massive data breach. Hey, I was kidding about the first one—sticking your head in the sand like an ostrich is not really an option. So let's talk about what can be done to mitigate the cybersecurity risks of offshoring.

Step 1: Are We Offshoring or What?

I can't tell you how many times I've heard this chestnut from chief privacy officers (CPOs): "My company is not offshoring any of our data; in fact, we have an iron-clad policy that prohibits offshoring!"

Yeah, right.

The first step is admitting you have a problem—an offshoring problem, that is. That's why organizations need to figure out where, when, and how data offshoring could be happening. This will not be easy. Pixie dust and happy thoughts make Peter Pan fly, but they won't magically reveal your company's data winging off to a foreign country (or being seen and used by foreign-based individuals).

So you're just going to have to do this the hard way:

1. If a picture is worth a million bitcoins, you will definitely get your money's worth by conducting a *data flow audit* and creating a *data flow map*. The result will be a detailed portrait showing how data get from one place to another in your organization. Trust me, it will be worth the effort! You really do need to know what types of data are sloshing around in your network, where it is going, where it is being stored, and how and with whom it is being shared. Big plus now, a data flow map will pinpoint the existence of any data offshoring!

2. Asking the question, "Got Offshoring?" is a simple way to find out when and where offshoring is happening in an organization.

This can be done in a number of ways:

- Send an e-mail to all company vendors with two simple questions. First, ask if the vendor has any staff located offshore; second, ask if the vendor is using any offshore subcontractors. It goes without saying that a *Yes!* to either question merits a call between the vendor and the company's CISO.
- Ask your legal department to add a *No Offshoring Clause* to any new contracts with vendors (as well as those that come up for renewal). This clause essentially states that the company prohibits any offshoring of their data by vendors unless the company consents in advance. This is a great internal control because if a vendor is offshoring, their legal counsel will try to strike out the No Offshoring Clause, which will flag that the vendor is offshoring.
- Educate your business leaders about the cyber perils of offshoring, so they are aware of the risks. The leaders can then alert the CISO and legal counsel so that they are aware a vendor is offshoring and can begin working to mitigate any cyber or legal risks.

Step 2: Yes, We Are Offshoring—Let's Do a Risk Assessment!

You've done your homework on data offshoring (either by conducting a data flow audit or by e-mailing a survey to vendors) and are shocked to find your company's data is being accessed in six foreign countries. Yikes! Now what?

Simple. You either find a way to mitigate the cybersecurity risks or you shut down the offshoring of data.

Welcome to the wild and woolly world of cybersecurity risk analysis! A risk analysis should be conducted for *each instance* of data offshoring. The risk analysis should focus on teasing out the cybersecurity risks belonging to a particular vendor. However, it is also important to gauge the effectiveness of potential risk mitigation strategies; if risks are identified and a vendor can't correct them, that's a problem!

Following are basic cybersecurity practices a company should demand from all offshore vendors with access to company data:

- Effective *logical* controls, such as multifactor authentication and encryption
- Effective *physical* controls, such as locked doors, security guards, closed-circuit television surveillance, and the like
- Policies and procedures establishing a privacy and cybersecurity program
- Education programs for employees on basic cyber hygiene and the dangers of phishing and other social engineering attacks
- The appointment of a CISO and a CPO
- A password management policy that mandates the use of strong passwords and prohibits the use of reused passwords
- A process to timely install patches and antivirus software
- A data backup and recovery plan
- Purchased a cyber liability insurance policy from a triple-A-rated insurance company

The preceding items are the floor, not the ceiling, of what should be expected by vendors. This means the risk analysis should encompass more than just the basics; it should be constructed upon a bedrock of common standards understood by cyber leaders across the world in many different industries—in other words, a *cybersecurity framework*.

One of the best cybersecurity frameworks is published by the National Institute of Standards and Technology of the U.S. Department of Commerce. The *NIST Cybersecurity Framework* is the gold standard and covers five domains: identify, protect, detect, respond, and recover. So when you use NIST, you can be confident of covering your bases.

Now that you've created a risk assessment using the NIST framework, you can go about the business of evaluating your offshore vendors to see if they measure up. One way to do this is by sending your cybersecurity team to the offshore location to conduct interviews and walk-throughs. But if you don't have the staff or budget to perform an on-site review, another option is to convert the risk analysis framework into a questionnaire to be answered by the vendor's CISO (or another knowledgeable representative).

The *Security Risk Assessment Questionnaire* (referred to as an *SRA*) can also ask for relevant documents, such as:

- Policies and procedures
- Educational materials
- Proof of cyber liability insurance
- Copies of third-party audits (such as SOC-2 security controls)

Once you receive the SRA from the vendor, the fun begins. Your CISO will need to evaluate the answers and review the documents to determine whether or not the offshore vendor should be allowed to have access to company data.

Certainly, if the vendor passes the review and gets good grades for having an effective cybersecurity program, then your CISO may very well approve data offshoring. Keep in mind, however, that a risk analysis is merely a snapshot in time. Therefore, it is important to do recurring risk analyses, perhaps annually, to ensure the vendor has maintained an effective cybersecurity program over time.

Now, remember when I said, Option 2 is to disallow or shut down data offshoring? Well, if the vendor flunks the risk assessment, and cannot or will not correct identified risks, then the CISO has to pull the plug on data offshoring. This must be done with all deliberate speed, as the risk of a cyberattack or data breach will be alarmingly high.

You should not allow any data offshoring when the vendor is:

- Not using encryption
- Not using strong passwords
- Not using multifactor authentication
- Reusing old passwords
- Not educating employees about phishing attacks
- Not installing patches

Furthermore, you should not allow any data offshoring when the vendor has:

- Poor physical controls, such as servers behind unlocked doors
- Poor or no data backup and recovery plan
- No cybersecurity policies
- No CISO or CPO

Any one of these internal control failures is a *big red flag* that should be addressed pronto before allowing data offshoring to proceed. Also, keep in mind that basic cybersecurity screw-ups like not using strong passwords usually come with a host of other cybersecurity screw-ups like not using 256-bit encryption or multifactor authentication.

The more cybersecurity screw-ups, the more it is likely the root cause is the vendor has no cybersecurity program. So when a vendor flunks your data offshoring risk analysis, it's best to walk away. Think of it like this. Vendors with no cybersecurity program are outright *enabling* cybercriminals to launch easy, successful, and destructive cyberattacks. So companies failing to conduct basic due diligence likely end up doing business with cyber-insecure vendors, increasing the probability of an offshore data breach. Why on earth would any company want to take this risk?

Step 3: Yes, We Are Offshoring—Can We Put That in Writing?

One of the most important cybersecurity controls to put in place is a companywide ban on data offshoring.

But wait, didn't I say a ban on data offshoring was probably doomed to fail?

Sure did, but here's the thing: prohibiting data offshoring is a great way to catch it before it happens!

I know, sounds like an oxymoron—but stay with me here for a moment. Once you know a vendor will be offshoring data, your CISO can do a risk assessment to see if offshoring data to this particular vendor is an acceptable risk; once a risk analysis has been completed, the company can decide whether or not to allow data offshoring.

To get the ball rolling, simply add a No Offshoring Clause to all vendor contracts that *prohibit data offshoring unless the company consents in advance.* The beauty of this strategy is it will catch data offshoring in the pre-contract vetting process with new potential vendors. It will also catch data offshoring with current vendors when their contract comes up for renewal.

Here's how it works:

1. The company's legal counsel provides a draft contract to a new vendor or a draft renewal contract with a current vendor.
2. The draft contract contains a clause, to the effect, "Vendor shall not offshore company data without the prior approval of the company."
3. The vendor's legal counsel strikes out the data offshoring prohibition and sends the draft contract back to company legal counsel.
4. Company legal counsel says, "Whoa! Why'd you strike out our data offshoring language?"
5. Vendor legal counsel responds, "Because we data offshore our butts off!"

Because data offshoring was flagged upfront, the company's CISO can conduct a risk assessment to advise whether or not to continue forward with the new vendor and allow data offshoring. If data offshoring is happening with a current vendor, then the CISO can conduct a risk assessment and work with the vendor to address any significant cybersecurity risks. A prohibition on data offshoring subject to company consent will be your greatest contractual tool to catch proposed data offshoring as well as data offshoring that's currently happening under your very nose.

Now let's say the company has uncovered data offshoring with a vendor and has conducted a cybersecurity risk assessment in which the vendor passed with flying colors.

Are we good to let data offshoring continue?

Not quite!

You've mitigated cybersecurity risk with operational and technical controls, which is great. But now you need to further mitigate these risks with cybersecurity controls embedded in your contracts with vendors.

These contractual mandates are very important, because there is no federal law in the United States that requires vendors to notify companies about data offshoring. Furthermore, many of the data privacy laws discussed in this book require the implementation of cybersecurity internal controls, but basically leave it up to companies to sweat the details. Therefore, companies must spell out their expectations around data offshoring in vendor contracts. This way the company and its vendors will be on the same page from the very beginning, and the consequences of failing to follow the contract will be clear to all.

As you begin to craft your strategy for managing the cybersecurity risks of data offshoring, I would offer a word of regulatory caution. This book is generally written to convey a wide scope of ideas regarding cybersecurity spanning many countries and industries. In crafting an approach to data offshoring, companies are well-advised to seek guidance from competent legal counsel to ensure compliance with the laws of their jurisdiction.

For example, it is important to determine whether there are laws in your country that require specific internal controls for, or outright prohibit, data offshoring. In addition, it is possible that contracts with government entities may regulate or prohibit data offshoring—for example, in the United States, some federal and state healthcare programs (e.g., Medicaid, Medicare Advantage) place restrictions on or prohibit the offshoring of beneficiary data. *Bottom line, a company might not be legally able to offshore its data, even if the risks are manageable.*

Managing the cybersecurity of data offshoring involves a patchwork of laws spanning the globe as well as the company's contracts with outside entities. So you'll need to bring your legal and cybersecurity folks together to hash out the legal barriers, risks, and solutions.

CHAPTER 11

Encryption Is the Ultimate Security Blanket

In prior chapters, we discussed the power of multifactor authentication, or MFA, as a backup measure to bolster an enterprisewide password management policy that hardwires the use of strong passwords and bans reusing passwords. We also discussed a company's most powerful asset—its employees—as the bulwark countermeasure standing between cybercriminals and the company's computer network. A cyber-savvy workforce, steeped in the basics of cyber hygiene, is an organization's first and strongest line of defense against the onslaught of a ransomware attack or massive data breach.

But employees are not robots (at least, not yet!), and we mere mortals make mistakes. Sometimes…

- A cybercriminal successfully tricks an employee into revealing the login password.
- An employee shares the login password with other employees or a friend.
- A patch is not installed due to human error or because the company does not have a patch management process.
- Employees are using an app or device without the knowledge (or approval) of the IT department.
- A company laptop containing sensitive data is stolen from the back seat of an employee's car.
- While decommissioning old, non-active servers, an IT employee forgets to erase disks containing the personal data of the company's customers.

Yes, mistakes happen—and when they do, nothing beats the safety, well-being, and fine, fresh scent of encryption! Like a Thundershirt swaddling a puppy as pitch-black clouds bang the sky, encryption provides soothing relief that your data is safe, even when it falls into the hands of nasty cybercriminals.

Encryption is an extra layer of security protecting the company's data when the first and strongest line of defense, a company's employees, has been cracked. Think of encryption as serving the same purpose as MFA. MFA backs up a world-class password management policy (one that mandates strong passwords and bans reused passwords) and serves as an extra layer of security when phishing attacks are successful (because without the one-time numeric code, or second factor, a cybercriminal cannot access the network even if the password is compromised).

Encryption does the same thing; when employees make a security goof, encryption is the backstop preventing data from falling into the wrong hands. Done correctly, encryption sheathes data in an impenetrable force field blocking access by an *unauthorized user*—that is, someone who has no business looking at the data.

Encryption is a powerful anti-hacking tool. When data is encrypted, it cannot be accessed by cybercriminals, thus reducing the likelihood of a massive data breach or demand for ransom. So yes, employees are a company's first and best line of defense, but encryption is the rock-ribbed shortstop who saves the game when employees have dropped the ball.

So What, Exactly, Is Encryption?

Think of encryption as ransomware in reverse. Instead of a cybercriminal infecting your network with malware that encrypts your data and sets you up for a ransom demand, you'll beat cybercriminals to the punch by encrypting your data first—and locking out the bad guys—as part of an effective cybersecurity program.

You can encrypt pretty much anything—cellphones, laptops, databases, servers, and even software applications—you name it. Let's look at e-mail, for example. When you have e-mails in your inbox waiting to be opened, this is known as *data at rest*. You should always encrypt data at rest. However, once you open the e-mail, write a response, and press the send button, that e-mail is winging its way through cyberspace until it gets to its intended recipient. This is known as *data in transit*. You should also encrypt data in transit. When you encrypt both data at rest and data in transit, you have encrypted the whole enchilada!

Now, data at rest is typically encrypted by an algorithm known as the Advanced Encryption Standard (AES). The most secure protection for data at rest is *AES 256-bit encryption*, so-called because it has a key length of 256 bits, yielding an astronomical number of possible combinations for a cybercriminal to crack; in short, we'd all be dead and buried before seeing a successful brute force attack on AES 256-bit encryption.

On the other hand, *Transport Layer Security*, or TLS, is the protocol used to encrypt data that is racing down the infobahn. You've probably noticed a little padlock in the address bar of your browser when you're checking your bank accounts or buying something on Amazon. That padlock is letting you know that TLS is hard at work blocking cybercriminals from seeing the data you are transmitting, like credit card numbers or passwords.

And that, my dear C-suite leader, is as non-techy a crash course in encryption as you're ever likely to get. Now that we've got the geeky stuff out of the way, let's get legal!

A Crash Course in Encryption Law (What Fun!)

Let me be blunt: Companies are on the hook for breaches of unencrypted data. Don't get hung up on whether your country has a blatant *thou shalt encrypt* mandate versus a wishy-washy guideline etched in quicksand. Likewise, don't kid yourself into thinking data encryption swims in a shallow creek where you can wriggle off the hook with a tall tale and top-notch privacy counsel. Encrypt you must, because government regulators come down hard on companies when lost or stolen data is not encrypted.

Let me give you some examples.

A law in the United States that tackles encryption is the *Health Insurance Portability and Accountability Act*, or HIPAA, which requires healthcare organizations to safeguard *protected health information* (PHI). HIPAA doesn't flat out mandate encryption; instead, the law provides that encryption is an "addressable" mechanism to be used when appropriate.

If you find this confusing, don't worry—the use of encryption has been cleared up, once and for all, by the agency in charge of enforcing HIPAA, the U.S. Department of Health and Human Services Office for Civil Rights (OCR).

Circa 2013, the OCR provided the following guidance on the question, "Is the use of encryption mandatory in the Security Rule?"

> *No. The final Security Rule made the use of encryption an addressable implementation specification. See 45 CFR § 164.312(a)(2)(iv) and (e)(2)(ii). The encryption implementation specification is addressable, and must therefore be implemented if, after a risk assessment, the entity has determined that the specification is a reasonable and appropriate safeguard in its risk management of the confidentiality, integrity, and availability of e-PHI. If the entity decides that the addressable implementation specification is not reasonable and appropriate, it must document that determination and implement an equivalent alternative measure, presuming that the alternative is reasonable and appropriate. If the standard can otherwise be met, the covered entity may choose to not implement the implementation specification or any equivalent alternative measure and document the rationale for this decision.*

Seems like there's a lot to unpack in OCR's 125-word legalese, so I'll boil it down in two sentences: "Encryption is not mandated until a breach hits the fan. Then it's mandated." To prove my point, here are a few HIPAA settlements to illustrate what happens when a breach hits the fan with unencrypted data:

- In 2014, Concentra Health Services agreed to pay a fine of $1.7 million to settle HIPAA violations involving a stolen, unencrypted laptop.
- In 2017, Lifespan, a Rhode Island-based health system, agreed to pay a $1.04 million penalty to settle HIPAA violations involving the theft of an unencrypted laptop from an employee's car. "Laptops, cellphones, and other mobile devices are stolen every day, that's the hard reality," OCR Director Roger

Severino said in a statement. Severino added that encrypting mobile devices is the best protection to thwart identity thieves.

- In 2019, the University of Rochester Medical Center agreed to pay a $3 million penalty for a lost, unencrypted flash drive and a stolen, unencrypted laptop. The OCR issued a press release with the headline, "Failure to Encrypt Mobile Devices Leads to a $3 million HIPAA Settlement." "Because theft and loss are constant threats, failing to encrypt mobile devices needlessly puts patient health information at risk," OCR Director Roger Severino said in a statement. "When covered entities are warned of their deficiencies, but fail to fix the problem, they will be held fully responsible for their neglect."

Across the pond, the landmark *General Data Protection Regulation*, or GDPR, provides stiff fines and penalties to organizations that fail to protect the personal data of citizens of the European Union (EU). The privacy provisions of the GDPR are breathtaking, with EU citizens having a *right to be informed* and a *right to be forgotten* and even rights relating to automated decision making and profiling.

Following are the 27 EU member countries (in alphabetical order):

1. Austria
2. Belgium
3. Bulgaria
4. Croatia
5. Republic of Cyprus
6. Czech Republic
7. Denmark
8. Estonia
9. Finland
10. France
11. Germany
12. Greece
13. Hungary
14. Ireland

15. Italy
16. Latvia
17. Lithuania
18. Luxembourg
19. Malta
20. The Netherlands
21. Poland
22. Portugal
23. Romania
24. Slovakia
25. Slovenia
26. Spain
27. Sweden

You may notice the United Kingdom is not on the list. That's because the United Kingdom left the EU in January 2020; however, the GDPR has been incorporated into United Kingdom law.

Now, then: what about encryption? Well, to comply with the GDPR, organizations must use *appropriate safeguards* to protect personal data, and GDPR's Article 32, Security of Processing, gives encryption as an example of an appropriate safeguard to manage cybersecurity risks and protect data. But don't be lulled into thinking GDPR is wishy-washy about encryption: companies that don't encrypt their data should expect the EU to levy massive fines in the event of a breach.

I've just skimmed the surface of privacy laws that give a shout out to encryption, but there are many others—Canada's Personal Information Protection and Electronic Documents Act (PIPEDA), Denmark's Danish Data Protection Act (DDPA), the global Payment Card Industry Data Security Standard (PCI-DSS), and more from the United States, like the Federal Information Processing Standards (FIPS) and Gramm–Leach–Bliley Act (GLBA).

So let me bottom line this thing for you. Don't be overly fixated on the legal technicalities (and vagaries) of the many data encryption laws spanning the globe—the reality is, encrypt you must! Trust me, if there's a massive breach and the data was not encrypted, bet on your country's regulators to hit you on the noggin with the proverbial kitchen sink (which hurts more than throwing a book at you, but they'll do that too).

The Key to Encryption

In the physical world, a key is used to lock or unlock the place where you protect your valuables, such as a safe deposit box. Much like a physical key, an *encryption key* is used to lock or unlock your data (referred to as encryption and decryption, respectively). The encryption key is a random chain of bits (the smallest unit of information) and the longer the chain, the harder it is to crack the encryption code. So a 256-bit key, which is the industry standard, is very strong. It would take billions and billions of years for a cybercriminal using a brute force attack to crack the encryption code of a 256-bit key.

Keep in mind that passwords and encryption keys are not at all the same. An encryption key is a super long, random chain of bits used by a software program to encrypt data. Passwords, however, are generated and used by humans to access login accounts, like an online bank account or a work-from-home VPN portal.

Passwords have a lot of vulnerabilities: they can be weak and easy to guess, stolen in a phishing scam, posted on the Dark Web from a breach, used for multiple login accounts, and shared between individuals—in other words, passwords can be cracked, and that's why encryption keys, and not passwords, are used to encrypt data.

It's also why the encryption key must be kept secure at all costs! Yes, it will take many billions of years to crack a 256-bit encryption code, but if cybercriminals get their hands on the actual encryption key, it is game, set, and match. The cybercriminals win.

Encryption key management is of paramount importance and should include policies around the creation, use, and storage of keys. Crucially, *you should store your encryption key in a separate place from where your data is*. This means you never store the key in the database you are encrypting! If cybercriminals hack into the database and find the encryption key, you've just given them a gold-engraved invitation to exfiltrate and unencrypt your data. In that same vein, it's a really bad idea to store the encryption key on the very server that has the data.

Got cloud storage? Well, it's also a really bad idea to let the cloud provider manage your encryption keys. In the event of a data breach, it is your company, not the cloud provider, who will be held responsible.

And let's focus a bit on the encryption key itself. Like a mama grizzly protecting her cubs, you must safeguard the encryption key at all times. Storing the encryption key in a separate place from the data is not enough, because cybercriminals might break into the storage area as well. So you need to encrypt the encryption key with *another* encryption key, and then store the second encryption key in a new location.

Wait, what? A second encryption key to encrypt the encryption key? Do we really need to be that paranoid? I would proffer that, sadly, the global epidemic of ransomware is evidence that we do.

There are many other aspects of best-in-class encryption key management—such as using different keys for different systems, changing keys every once in a while, and so forth—which your CISO can explain to you (yes, that was a hint, C-suite leader!). The critical point is while encryption is an incredibly powerful anti-hacking countermeasure, it is not foolproof, and its weakest link is the encryption key. So guard the encryption keys like your company's life was on the line; in the event of a data breach, it may well be.

CHAPTER 12

Data Backup

Easy as 3-2-1

Cost-effective, dependable, and efficient, data backups nonetheless remain the pimply faced frogspawn of cybersecurity. Backup is a behind-the-scenes chore nobody thinks about until something bad happens. Then, when data is lost or stolen, company leaders think the IT department can flip a switch to *Make backups go* and transport the missing data right back to where it belongs (apologies to Captain Grebnedlog of the Pakled spaceship Mondor).

Backups get no love. Backing up data is a drain on budget dollars that could be used for cool tech like breach detection software that leverages artificial intelligence and machine learning. Man oh man, if I can squeeze out a few extra budget dollars, I've got my eyes on a predictive endpoint security platform enabled by blockchain technology that zaps cybercriminals to a crisp with photon torpedoes!

Backups get no love. Backing up data won't stop a cyberattack, so why all the fuss? We need to go on the offensive and throw our resources at prevention so we don't have a ransomware situation in the first place. And anyway, if a cyberattack leads to a massive data breach, we're still totally screwed—data backups won't help with that. Plus, if a cyberattack gets past our stalwart cybersecurity crew, well—we've set aside a few bucks for fines and penalties to tide us over until the dust settles. Now that I think of it, probably would be a good idea to up the coverage limits to our cyber liability policy....

Backups get no love, and that's a shame. Sure, backing up your data won't repel a cyberattack, but data backup is the quintessential counter-measure when ransomware shuts down a company's network and stops critical operations dead in its tracks. It may not be gee-whiz tech anymore, but data backups are vital for getting operations up and running when disaster strikes. No doubt ransomware is a gigantic risk, but it's not the only calamity we need to keep an eye on. Natural disasters like hurricanes and earthquakes, not to mention human-made tragedies like wars and chemical spills, are a proximate cause of network crashes and the operational disruption that follows.

Keep in mind that business continuity is not about surviving a one-off event. Natural and man-made disasters are a fact of life, and it is a metaphysical certitude that ransomware cyberattacks are never going to fade away into the sunset. This means organizations must be in a constant state of readiness to restore their systems and operations to the point before the disaster struck. When the chips are down and disaster strikes at the heart of a business, it is backup that restores the blood, sinew, and soul of the company back to the pink of health.

Backups are beautiful! Let me count the ways.

- When ransomware encrypts a company's data, it is backups to the rescue, restoring the network to its pre-attack vim and vigor.
- When a flash flood sweeps away a cluster of servers, backups perform mouth-to-mouth, breathing new life into the company's network.
- When an employee obliterates mission-critical files, backups bring the once rotting data back to life.
- When a software patch crashes the network, backups are on call, stitching the network to its pre-crash condition.
- When that smoky, copper-smelling odor is wafting from a laptop, backups arrive at the scene to resuscitate the data that were heretofore lost to the flames.

Now that we've established the importance of data recovery as part of a cybersecurity program, let's get to know backups a little better. In simple terms, backups are the place where you store critical data so that the company's operations can be restored to their previous state. Backups that are *local*—meaning copies of data are stored onsite—include in-house servers, hard drives, tape drives, and USB flash drives. Data can also be stored offsite, in servers outside of the company's network, called *cloud backups*.

Restoring company data to its pre-disaster condition is as easy as 1-2-3 with the *3-2-1 backup rule*:

- *Spread the wealth!* Make sure you *keep three copies of the data*, this way critical data won't be annihilated by a single catastrophe, so that would be the original data, plus two backups, in case one or more copies get destroyed, lost, or stolen.
- *Don't keep all your eggs in one basket! Store the data in at least two different media* (e.g., hard drive, tape drive, cloud, etc.). This saves the day when there is a problem with one of the storage formats (e.g., hard drive crashes or cloud storage is down).
- *Location, location, location! Keep one copy offsite* as a safeguard when a disaster (e.g., fire, flood, cyberattack, etc.) destroys the backups at the onsite location.

No matter what misfortune befalls—be it human error, cyberattack, hardware crash, or natural disaster—the 3-2-1 rule will have your back, by bringing the company's data back, to the place in time before the calamity struck.

But we do have one gargantuan fly in the ointment. Cybercriminals know if a company has data backups, then the data can be restored even after a ransomware attack has encrypted the network, thus negating the likelihood that a fat, juicy ransom will be forthcoming. So, naturally, cybercriminals have caught on and are attacking the backups before they go after the network!

That's why it's important for companies to consider *air-gapped backups* on top of taking the 3-2-1 backup rule to heart. With air-gapped backups, company data is stored offline, meaning it's physically separate from the company's network. Air-gapped backups may be especially important for critical infrastructure companies like utilities and pipelines in the age of ransomware.

Certainly, not all organizations will have the financial wherewithal to bolster the 3-2-1 rule with air-gapped backups. Many other organizations will have the budget but not the will, concluding the cyberattack risk is not sufficient to justify implementing a *3-2-1-1 backup rule* (with the fourth *1* being an air-gapped backup).

Consider though the cataclysmic aftermath of a ransomware attack that encrypts both the organization's network and its backups. For a hospital unable to restore its electronic medical record, this could mean the medical histories of thousands of patients are lost forever. Or, a Fintech's data processing services could be disrupted globally, and maybe even permanently, impacting millions of customers.

How do you restore the organization's data to its pre-attack state, bring the network back online, and resume operations when you have no backup because the backup is encrypted by ransomware?

Maybe, you can't. Ever.

Now, do you think 3-2-1-1 backup is worth a second look?

CHAPTER 13

All Eyes on Social Media

A company's brand is one of its most valuable assets, which makes a company's social media presence a tempting bullseye for cybercriminals. It's no wonder cybercriminals circle the waters of social media like sharks hunting for prey. Social media platforms like Facebook, YouTube, Twitter, Instagram, Tik Tok, and LinkedIn are fertile ground for cybercriminals seeking to destroy a company's reputation to promote a political cause, obtain a ransom demand, or have a little fun. Social media is not just a headache for organizations; a company's employees can be stalked, threatened, blackmailed, or violently attacked by cybercriminals in pursuit of a social media scam or cyberattack.

Social media cyberattacks are abundant and hard to defend against because social media is so pervasive in people's lives. Pretty much everyone has some type of social media account, and it is this injection of social media into our personal and professional lives that creates arguably the largest threat vector in cybersecurity. Social media is under us, on top of us, between us, and inside of us; our most intimate thoughts and wildest fantasies spring alive in digital form, online, in real time, forever. The social media threat vector is as large as cyberspace; indeed, its sheer massiveness draws in cybercriminals like planets orbiting the sun.

Because social media platforms never sleep, and the greed of cybercriminals is endless, companies must galvanize their workforce for a 24/7/365 all-hands-on-deck struggle to repel social media scams and cyberattacks. Leading this struggle will be the organization's cybersecurity and marketing teams, working with leadership stakeholders, to devise a companywide strategy to implement social media policies, workforce education, and monitoring best practices to keep the cybercriminals at bay.

No doubt about it, social media is the backbone of marketing. Most organizations, regardless of size or budget, use social media to promote their brand and cultivate a meaningful bond with customers. Likewise, social media is a popular way for individuals to launch a business, land a dream job, make friends, or find true love.

Social media's ground-breaking data analytics and global reach to an audience numbering in the billions has redefined how human beings connect with each other. On the other hand, social media is a blazing sun orbited by con artists who ply their schemes with impunity on unsuspecting victims. So slather on some sunscreen and put on a wide-brimmed hat, as we take a deep dive into the many ways to get burned by social media scams.

Battered by Brandjacking

Cringe at the audacity of a political activist launching a counterfeit Twitter account with replicas of your company's logo to promote activities contrary to your brand. Quake with fear when a nation-state threat actor steals employee photos, doctors them with salacious imagery, and posts them to your company's Instagram site. Gulp down your vomit when a cybercriminal hijacks your company's Facebook account and posts obscenity-laced hate speech. On second thought, you may just want to barf and get it over with.

Take the words *brand* and *hijacking*, and you get the mishmash *brandjacking*, which is masquerading as someone else to damage a company's brand or reputation. This can be done by hacking into the company's online social media account and taking it over, or by creating a fake account out of whole cloth and pretending to be a representative of the company.

Many big companies have been victims of brandjacking. In 2014, a Twitter user created a fake account under the guise of the global food conglomerate, Heinz. The Twitter user pretended to be an intern for Heinz and posted humorous tweets that eventually morphed into political statements.

In 2015, a Facebook user pretended to be a customer service representative for the big-box department store Target. The fake customer service representative interacted with actual Target customers, oftentimes in a curt and dismissive manner. This went on for 16 hours before Target got wind of it and shut down the account.

Brandjacking can tarnish a beloved brand and lead to the loss of faithful customers amidst a media donnybrook. Even when the crime is brought to light and the scheme is shuttered, the company can find itself a laughing stock. Ah, I see you're getting nauseated again; worry not, as there are several countermeasures to block the bane of brandjacking.

The first and most important thing to do, as always, is to make sure all of your social media accounts are protected by strong passwords that are never reused and secured with multifactor authentication. If you have a big marketing department with staff logging into social media accounts on a daily basis, make sure each and every one of them has their own individual password—no sharing!!!

Please take note of the triple exclamation points in the aforementioned sentence; while not grammatically correct, I trust the use of !!! is an attention-getter. But just in case the triple exclamation points don't get you riled up, maybe this one-sentence zinger will drive home the point with crystal clear lucidity: *For all social media accounts, marketing staff must log in with strong passwords that are never reused, never shared, and secured with multifactor authentication turned on!*

The second thing to do is monitor all the *mentions* that your social media generates. You should be checking tweets, likes and dislikes, comments, and emojis. This way, you'll find out quickly when someone is using the company's brand for nefarious purposes. If it takes 16 hours to uncover brandjacking, that's 16 hours' worth of damage to your brand. Think how many customers a cybercriminal can make hopping mad in 16 hours. As a social media blast can reach millions of people in seconds flat, time is of the essence in ferreting out brandjacking.

One way to monitor social media is by purchasing a *social listening tool*, which is software your marketing department can use to monitor any mentions about the company's brand across every social media platform. If you run a small business and can't afford a social listening tool, then you should assign staff to plant their eyeballs on the company's social media platforms, with a focus on customer feedback and complaints to product placements.

Another way to hijack a brand is by purchasing a domain name similar to that of a company but missing a letter or two. By misspelling the website name of a company, customers are directed to a fake website where they can be scammed or the company's brand can be maligned.

This is called *typosquatting* and is why many companies will purposely buy misspelled domain names. As a third countermeasure, be sure to buy domain names that are similar to the name of your company, so cyber-criminals can't buy a similar but misspelled domain name that directs your customers to a fake site. Keep in mind that *.com* is only one of many domain extensions; so you'll want to register your real domain name with multiple extensions, like *.store*, *.edu*, or *.org*, as applicable.

The fourth countermeasure is to preserve your legal rights by trade-marking your business. Trademarking can't physically stop a brandjacking attack, but it affords another cause of action in a lawsuit. At the very least, the potential to be on the business end of a trademark infringement complaint will make someone think twice about brandjacking your company.

Decimated by Disgruntled Employees

Current and former employees can do tremendous damage to a company's brand when they vent their frustrations on social media platforms. Employees with a deep personal connection to their employer may become disgruntled and go off the rails because:

- They are not emotionally ready to accept the loss of a job, whether due to companywide layoffs or the result of their own misconduct.
- Anger at management sets their fingers pounding away on a keyboard with flaming comments posted to Facebook or Twitter.
- Employees who have political or philosophical disagreements with a company policy may be inspired to post their concerns to a social media platform.

Whatever the reason for employee discontent, organizations need to monitor social media platforms (presumably with a social listening tool) to be on the lookout for mentions by employees. But what, exactly, can organizations do when an employee posts damaging comments on social media? Is it as simple as asking the employee to remove the negative post?

The answer will depend on the laws of your country. In the United States, Section 7 of the *National Labor Relations Act* affords workers "the right to self-organization, to form, join, or assist labor organizations, to bargain collectively through representatives of their own choosing, and to engage in other concerted activities for the purpose of collective bargaining or other mutual aid or protection."

The federal agency charged with enforcing U.S. labor laws, the National Labor Relations Board (NLRB), has opined "This protection extends to certain work-related conversations conducted on social media, such as Facebook and Twitter."

So asking an employee to delete the damaging post could land a company in hot water under Section 7 of the National Labor Relations Act. For example, if the employee is posting on Facebook about pay or benefits, that is likely to be protected speech, and the company could be viewed as attempting to trample on the employee's rights under the act. In addition, if the employee works for the federal government, the social media post could be free speech protected under the First Amendment to the U.S. Constitution.

Bottom line, organizations will need to consult with legal counsel to craft a social media policy that meets the laws of their country. In the United States, a social media policy must meet the National Labor Relations Act, as well as other federal and state laws.

When in doubt, perhaps the best approach is for the company's marketing department to simply post a rebuttal to the employee's negative social media comments. The company's rebuttal should be polite and make it clear the employee does not speak for the company, and that the company will investigate the concerns raised, if warranted.

Can't Un-See That

TMI, people! Snapping photos of employees at a company event and posting to Facebook may be a great morale booster, but it's also a source of *social media intelligence* for cybercriminals planning a cyberattack.

For example, if employees are wearing their company badges in a photo, a cybercriminal could use their names and job titles to send phishing e-mails to the department. Or, cybercriminals could use the photo to create fake badges and piggyback their way into a restricted area. Or, if the team is posing in front of a whiteboard scribbled with sensitive company data, the information might alert the cybercriminal to a control vulnerability that could be exploited.

Putting *too much information* in social media posts is a tremendous risk for organizations, but it can also place employees in grave danger. Employees often compromise themselves by posting personal information such as dates of birth, names of children, places worked, or colleges attended. This information can be tracked by cybercriminals who can put all the pieces together to commit crimes against the employees themselves. A cybercriminal could steal the identity of an employee to fraudulently apply for a credit card or to create a fake purchase order to bilk goods from a company vendor.

This is why your cybersecurity awareness program needs to include a module on the dangers of social media. Employees should be warned about the kinds of cybercrimes that could happen when they are not careful about posting personal information.

Employees should be instructed not to wear their badges in company photos and to be wary of whiteboards or other information in the background that could be used by cybercriminals for nefarious schemes. Finally, employees should be cautioned not to share details that could make them a target of a cybercriminal, like dates of birth, work and home addresses, phone numbers, and license plate numbers.

A *Take Care, Don't Share* social media awareness program is a potent countermeasure against cyberattacks and is a public service that enhances the personal safety of company employees. Every company should be doing this.

CHAPTER 14

Culture Eats Cybercriminals for Lunch

A company's most powerful line of defense against ransomware is a cyber-savvy workforce; conversely, employees asleep at the switch are easy pickings for wily cybercriminals looking for a quick score. Employees can be a wrought iron shield defending the organization from earth-shattering cyberattacks, or they can be the soft, white underbelly cybercriminals rip to shreds with malware and phishing scams.

You've probably heard the saying, "Culture eats strategy for lunch." Well, in the age of ransomware, and with apologies to Peter Drucker, I would say it's more like "A culture of cybersecurity eats hackers for lunch!"

That's why instilling a culture of cybersecurity throughout the organization is so important to preventing a cyberattack or a data breach. A culture of cybersecurity is the fuel that will turbocharge your employees into a workforce of cyber warriors ready to smack down whatever cybercriminals throw at them.

Cybersecurity sounds intimidating, but employees don't need to be techno-geeks to understand basic cyber hygiene. The trick is to create a cybersecurity program focusing on the real-life cyber threats employees will face in both their personal and professional lives. Stay grounded on basic cyber hygiene; complicated, esoteric gobbledygook should be avoided like the plague!

Keep in mind the weakest link in your organization will be a human being, not a computer or software program. This means people, not technology, should be the main focus of a strong cybersecurity program. A people-focused workplace, *where employees buy into and are engaged with cybersecurity*, will be a rock-bottom risk profile for cyberattacks and a diamond-hard target for cybercriminals.

Don't Let Passwords Bring You Down!

Everybody in the world, heck—maybe even the universe—uses passwords to log in to their online accounts, so this should be a pretty easy layup for your cybersecurity training program, right? Well, maybe not. Problem is, too many people use weak passwords, reused passwords, and even shared passwords—crikey, it's a jungle out there!

Abysmal password security is the number one threat to an organization, so it's important to steep the workforce in basic password hygiene with tips and tricks embedded in the training:

- Always use strong passwords that are hard to guess. Use a combination of letters, numbers, and symbols, and the longer the better. An example would be *$Y8e37%he4y#73U*.
- A strong password can also be a long *passphrase* that's easy for you to remember but unique enough that it can't be easily guessed. An example of a passphrase would be *Yikes4tentsfelldownlastaugust!*.
- Never use passwords that are easy to guess, such as password123, iloveyou, qwerty, or 12345678.
- Never use any personal information in your passwords, such as your name, friend's name, pet's name, or date of birth.
- Do not use one password for many different accounts or different devices. Every account and device must have its own, unique password.
- Change your passwords every 60 days. If you believe your password has been lost or stolen, change your password immediately and contact the cybersecurity department.
- Never reuse a password. All passwords must be new and unique.
- Do not share passwords with anyone, such as your supervisor or co-workers.
- Use multifactor authentication as an extra layer of security to prevent unauthorized access to your account in case a password has been lost or stolen.

Training the workforce on password hygiene will help safeguard the organization from a cyberattack and is a public service that will benefit employees in their personal life. And when it comes to cybersecurity, who doesn't love a win–win?

Phishing: Don't Get Reeled In!

An organization is only one stolen password away from a disastrous cyberattack. Cybercriminals are skilled in social engineering techniques to deceive employees into divulging their usernames and passwords. Coupled with an enterprisewide password management policy, multifactor authentication is a powerful defense against phishing and brute force attacks. But even multifactor authentication is not unhackable.

No defense is foolproof, and cybercriminals are always looking for cybersecurity workarounds. Worse, the odds are in the bad guy's favor; all it takes is one phished employee to bring a company to its knees.

That's why a company's first and best line of defense is its workforce. Phishing attacks are an existential threat to any business, so it's crucial to train employees so that they can easily spot a fake phishing e-mail. A cyber-savvy workforce is more than a match for the best cybercriminals— even politically motivated state-sponsored threat actors can be thwarted by employees who are on their toes.

First up, don't assume your workforce even knows that phishing attacks are possible. You'd be surprised by the number of people who don't know phishing even exists. Many other employees are vaguely aware of phishing but are focused (or stressing out) on other things in life—like churning out a critical report under a tight deadline.

So it's important to start with basic phishing awareness training, and every so often remind the workforce to keep phishing in their sights as they go about their daily work routines. One way to keep the workforce on their toes is with *internal phishing campaigns*. Fake e-mails are sent by the cybersecurity department to phish employees by tricking them to click on a link. If the employee clicks on the link, a friendly reminder pops up to educate the employee about the dangers of phishing attacks.

In addition to basic phishing awareness, it is important to train employees on how to spot a fake e-mail. Phishing attacks can be stopped by vigilant employees on the lookout for tell-tale signs that something *phishy* is going on:

- Is the e-mail from someone you know in the organization?
- Where is the e-mail coming from? Is the e-mail address external to the organization?
- Does the e-mail ask you to provide your username and password, or any other personal information?
- Does the e-mail contain spelling and grammatical errors?
- Does the e-mail ask you for money?
- Does the e-mail ask for an urgent, immediate task to be completed?
- Does the e-mail ask that documents or data be provided to a government investigator or agency?
- Does the e-mail contain threatening language?
- Does the e-mail state that your "account has been suspended"?
- Does the e-mail contain an odd attachment?
- Is there something weird or suspicious about the e-mail?

In addition to the red flags of phishing, a good phishing awareness campaign will warn employees to never provide their username and password in response to an e-mail. There should also be a policy that the company will never ask for an employee's username and password via e-mail—and this policy should be clearly communicated to the workforce. Finally, employees should be cautioned to never click on links or attachments unless absolutely certain the e-mail is safe.

Once employees are trained to spot a phishing scam, they can report the fake e-mail to the company's cybersecurity department. This can be done by purchasing an *anti-phishing platform* allowing employees to report fake e-mails with the click of a button.

Cofense *Report Fish* and Proofpoint *PhishAlarm* are popular anti-phishing platforms with handy *Report Phishing* buttons that are added to the e-mail toolbar for quick and easy reporting. Once the employee clicks on the button, the suspected phishing e-mail is sent to the cybersecurity department for safe analysis and is deleted from the employee's e-mail account.

One last thing—even with an extensive phishing campaign and a high-grade anti-phishing platform, mistakes will happen and employees will get scammed. So, you want to let your employees know when mistakes happen, they should immediately change their password and report the incident to the cybersecurity team. You also want to establish a *just culture* of not punishing honest mistakes but instead consoling the employee and ensuring the problem is fixed. Instilling fear and shame will lead to unreported phishing attacks that do not get blocked and could lead to a data breach or a devastating ransomware cyberattack.

Guarding the Gates With Physical Security

Ransomware seems born from a cybernetic netherworld of phishing scams and zero-day attacks, but cybercriminals are not ghosts in the machine; they are human beings (I strongly suspect) who live in the physical world, just like you and I. That's why cybersecurity training programs must hone in on real-world dangers, not just those existing in cyberspace. Otherwise, sneaky cybercriminals will leave employees writhing in the dust.

Here's the worst that could happen:

- An employee is completely oblivious to the stranger sneaking in behind as the employee badges into a restricted area (a trick known as *tailgating*).
- That same employee is later tricked by a cybercriminal claiming to be a building inspector who requests access to an area that is off-limits, such as the data center where servers are housed (a hack known as *piggybacking*).
- An employee logging into a computer is snooped on by a co-worker observing slit-eyed as the password is keyed in (this nosy pursuit is *shoulder surfing*).
- An employee carelessly throws out files containing sensitive data, which are fished out of the trash by a cybercriminal and used to create a phishing attack against the company (this downright dirty activity is *dumpster diving*).

- An employee stumbles upon a USB drive on the tarmac of
  the office parking lot, and thinking it belongs to a co-worker,
  inserts the USB drive into a computer, where it uploads a
  crypto worm infecting the network with ransomware
  (the infamous *USB drop attack*).
- An encrypted laptop is stolen from an employee's car in a
  smash and grab; affixed to the laptop is a bright yellow sticky
  note scribbled with the encryption password because, in the
  employee's own words, "I made the password so strong I
  could never remember it."

Everyone makes mistakes, but the biggest blunder of all is not having
a conversation with your workforce about physical security—talk about
it till you're blue in the face; talk about it till the cows come home; talk
about it till the sun doesn't shine; then, when you're all poured out, talk
about it some more!

To get the conversation started, here are some hands-on things everyone can do to keep the workplace safe and cyber secure:

- **Lock up your devices!** Portable devices such as laptops and
  cellphones are easy to steal, so never leave them unattended,
  and always lock them up when not in use.
- **Lock the laptop in your trunk!** Never leave a laptop on your
  car seat for criminals to steal. Always keep your laptop locked
  in your trunk.
- **Clean up your desk!** Do not place sticky notes on your
  devices or in your work area that contain sensitive information, such as your password. Do not leave confidential
  documents or removable media (e.g., USB drives, CDs,
  cellphones, etc.) laying around your workspace as they are
  tempting targets for thieves. Lock up all sensitive materials
  and devices when you leave your workspace.
- **Beware of dumpster divers!** Do not throw out confidential
  documents in the trash. Documents containing sensitive
  information, such as financial or medical data, must be
  disposed of in the shredder bin.

- **No tailgating allowed!** Watch out for anyone trying to sneak in behind you when entering a restricted area.
- **Don't give piggyback rides!** Be on the lookout for swindlers trying to con you into giving them access to a restricted area. When in doubt, call security to check them out.
- **Say no to shoulder surfing!** Make sure no one can see you typing your password when you log in to your computer.
- **Careful—the USB stick could be a trick!** Never plug unapproved removable media (e.g., USB drives, CDs, etc.) into a computer because it may contain malware. Only use company-approved removable media and devices. Report all unapproved media to the cybersecurity department immediately.

Wi-Fi Spoofing

When working from home, it's not unusual to get cabin fever and set up shop at the mythical third place (a locale that is not your workplace and not your home)—it'd be nice if it was Shangri-La, but most likely you're sitting in a Starbucks with a heady caffeine buzz as your laptop connects to public Wi-Fi.

Employees work everywhere these days, be it a coffee shop, while traveling by train or bus, stopped for an airport layover, or hunkering down in a hotel room. And, at every location, there is free public Wi-Fi.

Unfortunately, public Wi-Fi presents a real danger for employees on the go. In a *Wi-Fi spoofing* attack, instead of connecting to the coffee shop Wi-Fi access point, the employee unwittingly joins the cybercriminal's Wi-Fi access point, or *Evil Twin*. Once connected to the evil twin access point, the victim's device is directed to a fake public Wi-Fi landing page that looks like the real Wi-Fi landing page of a coffee shop, hotel lobby, or other location where the employee is working. Now, everything the employee types on this *Evil Portal* is seen and documented by the cybercriminal—usernames, passwords, and any other login information—it's all in the hands of the cybercriminal now!

My advice is to provide work-from-home and traveling employees with a virtual private network (VPN), then mandate they can only connect to public Wi-Fi if they use the company-provided VPN. A VPN sends and receives information via an encrypted tunnel and keeps all the data private. With a VPN, nobody can see what the employee is typing, looking at, working on, or doing. A VPN is the only secure way of connecting to a public Wi-Fi network.

The best things in life are free, but not when it's public Wi-Fi! So make sure cybersecurity awareness training addresses how to be safe when using public Wi-Fi.

- **Only connect to secure Wi-Fi!** Only use Wi-Fi from a trusted source with a secure network (typically requires a password/registration and is encrypted).
- **The less said and done the better!** Do not shop online, access bank accounts, use credit cards, or conduct sensitive company business when using free public Wi-Fi.
- **Only browse encrypted websites!** Only visit encrypted websites that begin with *HTTPS*. Never visit websites that begin with *HTTP*.
- **VPN is the way to go!** Whenever possible, use the company's VPN when connecting to public Wi-Fi.

CHAPTER 15

The C-Suite Gets Sacked

What happens when a cyberattack causes a massive data breach or shuts down a network affecting millions of people? Well, it makes the news for one thing. Lawsuits fly. The FBI launches an investigation. Congressional hearings ensue. Oh, and C-suite executives lose their jobs.

- Target's CEO and CIO resigned in the aftermath of a 2014 breach impacting up to 110 million Target customers. Cybercriminals infiltrated Target's network using stolen login credentials from a third-party vendor that provided refrigeration and HVAC services to Target stores.
- The co-chair of Sony Pictures Entertainment resigned after a 2015 breach in which cybercriminals released embarrassing e-mails to the public.
- The Director of the U.S. Office of Personnel Management resigned after a 2015 cyberattack in which cybercriminals tricked their way into a database containing personnel records on over 21 million people.
- Equifax's CEO, CIO, and CISO stepped down after a 2017 cyberattack—one that could have been avoided by patching a software vulnerability—resulted in a massive data breach affecting nearly 143 million Americans.

Breaches and cyberattacks are widely reported in the news, particularly when the data breach is massive or the cyberattack impacts critical infrastructure. Let's face it, when ransomware shuts down a U.S. pipeline, the resulting fuel shortages and price hikes are going to be newsworthy. It should come as no surprise that news media will be particularly harsh when cybercriminals succeeded because a company failed to take simple cybersecurity precautions. Companies that did not retire unused VPNs, or did not enable multifactor authentication, or failed to patch known software vulnerabilities—well, they got some splainin' to do!

Yes, it's true the actual victim here is the company that was hacked and the real bad guys are, well, the cybercriminals who launched the cyberattack. But C-suite executives should not be surprised—and in fact, should *expect*—that the media will excoriate companies in the wake of massive data breaches or destructive ransomware attacks.

Take a gander at these headlines and you'll get the picture:

Equifax to pay $700 million for massive data breach. Here's what you need to know about getting a cut (CNBC Make It, July 22, 2019)

Capital One Reports Data Breach Affecting 100 Million Customers, Applicants (*The Wall Street Journal*, July 29, 2019)

Neglected Server Provided Entry for JPMorgan Cybercriminals (*The New York Times*, December 22, 2014)

Colonial Pipeline CEO Tells Why He Paid Cybercriminals a $4.4 Million Ransom (*The Wall Street Journal*, May 29, 2021)

Cybercriminals Breached Colonial Pipeline Using Compromised Password (Bloomberg, June 4, 2021)

Data of more than 40 million exposed in T-Mobile breach (*Los Angeles Times*, August 18, 2021)

Morgan Stanley settles personal data breach lawsuit for $60 million (*The Washington Post*, January 3, 2022)

And why shouldn't the media be harsh? Consider how a data breach could affect millions of innocent people who had nothing to do with the cyberattack in the first place. The nearly 143 million Americans impacted by the Equifax breach deserve to be sorely vexed. A simple software update to correct a widely known vulnerability would have stopped the cyberattack dead in its tracks. But Equifax didn't install the darn patch.

Not installing software updates is a careless mistake that just gets people rip-snorting, crazy mad! Yes, the cybercriminals are the bad guys, and we want them to go to jail, but when companies drop the ball on basic cyber hygiene and millions of innocent people get hurt, that's an epic management failure, leading to righteous, justifiable public anger.

Recall the discussion in Chapter 1 about the convergence of operational technology (OT) and information technology (IT), where operational technologies that *physically do something* (like software that monitors or controls fuel valves in a pipeline) are enmeshed with informational technologies that *manage data* (like computers, servers, and software applications). You see this a lot in critical infrastructure companies such as utilities, pipelines, and water treatment plants because the upside to IT/OT convergence is fine-tuned, streamlined operations, and real-time data analytics.

But the downside is, well, potentially nightmarish. OT systems connected to the Internet are vulnerable to cyberattacks, potentially causing tremendous social, financial, and physical damage.

- A nation-state threat actor could shut down a country's power grid, turning off lights and heat for thousands or even millions of citizens. If such an attack occurred during sub-zero temperatures in the wintertime, it would be a life-threatening event.
- A nation-state threat actor could also hack into an agricultural drone that is used by a farmer to monitor soil composition. Once the hacker has control, the drone could be ordered to slam into a police station or a hospital. Or, a swarm of hacked drones could ram into an oil refinery, spilling deadly fuel and toxic chemicals.
- Cybercriminals could change the concentration of benign chemicals at a water treatment plant, turning the drinking water into a toxic beverage not safe for human consumption.
- A cybercriminal with a grudge could take control of an autonomous vehicle and drive it remotely to run over an ex-spouse or co-worker. A truly unhinged cybercriminal could commandeer the autonomous vehicle to smash into a crowd at a festival or crash into a day care center, killing babies and toddlers.

These scenarios are frightening and sadly very plausible. If someone dies from a hack—particularly a hack preventable by basic cyber hygiene—the company will be blamed for the ensuing damage as much as the cybercriminals.

When cyberattacks strike, C-suite leaders should expect a firestorm of negative public opinion amid withering media scrutiny and a flurry of government investigations. They should expect stiff fines and penalties.

They should expect huge payouts to victims and class-action lawsuits. And C-suite executives should expect to lose their jobs.

The accountability for successful cyberattacks falls squarely on the shoulders of the C-suite, and by this, I mean the chief executive officer (CEO), chief financial officer (CFO), chief operations officer (COO), and the chief information officer (CIO). However, if you are a company leader and you don't see your title on this list, do not rejoice. I am also pointing a finger at YOU if you have a leadership role where you make companywide operational decisions impacting cybersecurity. Companies have varied leadership roles with a myriad of titles and responsibilities, so there is no one-size fits all rule for accountability. Bottom line, whatever the role or title, the most senior executive leaders in the company are accountable for implementing an effective cybersecurity program.

Gone are the days when a top leader, such as the CEO or CFO, could escape accountability by pinning the blame on other, lower-ranking executives. The *Sarbanes–Oxley Act of 2002* (SOX) rose from the ashes of accounting scandals involving publicly traded companies that at the time were household names, such as Enron Corporation, WorldCom, and Tyco International. The raison d'etre of SOX is to protect company shareholders from fraudulent financial reporting, and one key way SOX does this is by requiring company CEOs and CFOs to certify the financial records "comply with SEC disclosure requirements and fairly present in all material aspects the operations and financial condition of the issuer."

And SOX has teeth. CEOs and CFOs who sign off on financial statements they know are not accurate can go to jail.

SOX is focused on the accuracy of financial statements and the internal controls around a company's financial reporting; SOX does not specifically zero in on cybersecurity. However, in today's digital age, the vast majority of financial workflows rely on information technology such as databases, accounting software, and servers—all of which are potentially vulnerable to data breaches and ransomware attacks. CEOs and CFOs should take note that cyber risk related to the information technology used in financial recordkeeping is fair game under SOX.

While there is a cybersecurity angle with SOX, its scope is limited to information technology solely related to financial recordkeeping and reporting. However, cybersecurity has become an area of intense focus for the Security and Exchange Commission (SEC), which in 2018 issued a *Commission Statement and Guidance on Public Company Cybersecurity Disclosures* to help publicly traded companies in disclosing cybersecurity risks and cyber incidents.

The SEC guidance, perhaps reflecting on the convergence of OT and IT—that is, the merging of physical operations with digital technology—warns that "companies face an evolving landscape of cybersecurity threats in which cybercriminals use a complex array of means to perpetrate cyber-attacks, including the use of stolen access credentials, malware, ransomware, phishing, structured query language injection attacks, and distributed denial-of-service attacks, among other means."

Successfully hacked companies, though they are the victim, may find themselves reeling from a number of undesirable outcomes, according to the SEC guidance:

1. **Remediation costs** for things like damage to systems or compensation to customers affected by the cyberattack.
2. **Cybersecurity costs** to shore up the company's cyber defenses, such as hiring cybersecurity staff, training the workforce, or purchasing cybersecurity protection technologies.
3. **Lost revenues** due to losing customers and business partners after a cyberattack.
4. **Litigation and legal risks** from state and federal investigations or the imposition of substantial fines and penalties.
5. **Insurance premiums** increase.
6. **Reputational damage** and loss of confidence
7. **Damage to competitiveness**, stock price, and long-term shareholder value.

The SEC guidance emphasizes the importance of companies developing cybersecurity risk management policies and procedures. If company management doesn't perform cybersecurity risk assessments and tabletop exercises, they won't know what cyber risks even exist; this leads to inadequate disclosure and reporting of potential cybersecurity risks.

Lack of management controls to spot cyber risks may lead to claims of negligence and management liability in the event of a successful cyberattack. Policies should be in place to ensure cyber risks are reported up the chain of command to the appropriate division leaders and senior executives who will be making important decisions about cybersecurity operations, disclosures of risk, and how cyber incidents are handled.

The SEC guidance also prohibits executives from trading company stock if they are aware of cybersecurity incidents and opines on the importance of disclosing the board's role in overseeing material cybersecurity risk.

With the subtlety of a sledgehammer, the SEC has woven management accountability into each and every paragraph of the 24-page guidance document. CEOs and other senior management cannot escape personal liability by pointing fingers at the CIO or CISO. Top management at publically traded companies is expected to have policies and controls in place to identify cyber risk and disclose risks and incidents to investors and the SEC.

In fact, the SEC's *2020 Division of Enforcement Annual Report* called out individual accountability as critical to the effectiveness of its enforcement program and—with perhaps more than an ounce of pride—said, "In Fiscal Year 2020, the Commission charged individuals in 72 percent of the standalone enforcement actions it brought. Those charged include individuals at the top of the corporate hierarchy, including numerous CEOs and CFOs, as well as accountants, auditors, and other gatekeepers."

In January 2020, the SEC released a 13-page report on *Cybersecurity and Resiliency Observations*. While recognizing there is no one-size fits all approach to cybersecurity, the report offered seven best practices companies can use to enhance cybersecurity and improve operational resiliency:

1. **Governance and risk management:** Policies to ensure that senior leaders and the board are engaged in cybersecurity, conducting assessments to identify cyber risk, and monitoring of the effectiveness of cyber policies and controls
2. **Access rights and controls:** Controls around user access and access management
3. **Data loss prevention:** Procedures to ensure that data is not lost, stolen, or compromised
4. **Mobile security:** Policies to secure mobile devices and applications

5. **Incident response and resiliency:** Development of incident response plans, corrective action plans, and planning to recover from a cyber incident

6. **Vendor management:** Due diligence for selecting vendors, as well as monitoring to ensure vendors meet cybersecurity requirements

7. **Training and awareness:** Training the workforce on the company's cybersecurity policies as well as specific risks such as phishing.

By now you should get the message: the SEC holds company leaders accountable for cybersecurity. But just in case C-suite leaders decide to plant their heads in the sand, in March 2022 the SEC issued a proposed rule on *Cybersecurity Risk Management, Strategy, Governance, and Incident Disclosure.* The proposed rule fortifies all the prior SEC cybersecurity rules and guidelines with the regulatory equivalent of an antibiotic: disclosure of all things related to cybersecurity governance, risk management, and incident reporting. When the SEC's proposed rule becomes final, it will represent a sea change in how public companies report on cybersecurity oversight and cyberattacks.

The SEC's proposed rule will protect investors by upping the ante in how publicly traded companies report cybersecurity matters. Specifically, the SEC proposal requires:

1. Disclosing material cyberattacks within 4 days of the incident
2. Periodic disclosures (via Form 10-K) regarding:
   - Policies and procedures to identify and manage cybersecurity risk
   - Management's role in implementing cybersecurity policies and procedures
   - Board of directors' cybersecurity expertise and its oversight of cybersecurity risk
   - Updates of previously reported cybersecurity incidents

And there you have it. The SEC has come a long way from powerful but oft-ignored guidance to in-your-face cybersecurity rulemaking that'll knock C-suite leaders on their butt if they don't comply. The fact is, senior leaders at publicly traded companies are on the hook for cybersecurity.

When the lights go out from a cyberattack, CEOs should not expect the CISO to take a bullet for the company because the bullet will just pass through the CISO's body right into the CEO's chest anyway.

While the focus of this chapter is on the SEC's approach to cybersecurity accountability, don't forget there are many state and federal agencies ready to take on corporate management over a cyberattack or massive data breach. There are also subpoena-wielding state attorney generals and an army of plaintiff attorneys ready to file money-spinning class-action lawsuits.

In 2019, Senator Elizabeth Warren (D., MA) introduced the Corporate Executive Accountability Act, which would impose criminal liability on C-suite executives when data breaches are caused by management negligence. Executives who violate the Corporate Executive Accountability Act could spend one year in jail for the first offense and up to three years in jail for a subsequent conviction.

So, don't expect the grassroots movement holding executives accountable for cyberattacks to abate anytime soon. On the contrary, you can expect C-suite accountability to be a colossal part of the equation whenever cyberattacks harm thousands or even millions of innocent people.

But accountability does not stop at the C-suite's door. Let's also not forget the role of the board of directors who are similarly privileged with fiduciary responsibility for the health and well-being of the company. An independent board of directors has ultimate oversight over cybersecurity and should expect the same type of negative publicity and personal liability as the C-suite leadership team.

CHAPTER 16

Mobilizing the C-Suite

Waging War Against Cyberattacks

An epidemic of cyberattacks is battering companies across the world. It seems like every day a cyberattack has shut down a computer network or hurled a massive pile of sensitive data into the eager hands of cybercriminals. It's no wonder CISOs are in high demand. But you can't just hire the best CISO on the planet and call it a day. Handing off cybersecurity to a great CISO will simply not cut it anymore. C-suite leaders, especially the CEO, are ultimately accountable for cybersecurity within the organization and could be held liable for damage caused by ransomware attacks or massive data breaches. As such, it is incumbent upon C-suite leaders to provide *engaged oversight* of the cybersecurity program. Engaged oversight means providing moral, and when necessary, political support to the CISO.

There will be times when a cybersecurity countermeasure, such as requiring strong passwords or enabling multifactor authentication (MFA), meets stiff resistance by department leaders or rank-and-file employees. Strong passwords might be opposed by employees who think logging in with all those crazy numbers, letters, and symbols is just too darn much extra work. Department leaders might believe turning on MFA slows their workflow down to a crawl resulting in missed deadlines. Whatever the pushback, C-suite executives must support the CISO to overcome mistaken barriers to implementing basic cyber hygiene.

Let's face it, basic cyber hygiene causes little, if any, extra work. Mandating strong passwords or enabling MFA will not bog down a department's operations, resulting in unfinished deliverables. Strong passwords and MFA are the quintessential *no-brainers*, and any organization failing to implement these cyber controls does so at its own peril.

Bottom line, support your CISO!

Another way that C-suite leaders can provide engaged oversight is by being a cybersecurity role model. C-suite leaders should realize they are always being watched and judged by their employees, colleagues, and business partners. A company's leadership team is under a white-hot spotlight 24/7/365. Eyes peeled like hawks in the sky hunting rabbits, company staff soak in everything about their leaders:

- Staff know when their leaders arrive in the office and when their leaders clock out for the day.
- Staff know the leaders who are habitually late to meetings versus the leaders who are conscientiously punctual.
- Staff know where their leaders went for lunch, with whom, who ate what, and how the CEO and CFO spilled wine on their shirts.
- Staff know when their leaders had a good day ("Sales are up!") or a very bad day ("Ugh—my best customer signed with another firm!").

But above all, staff have an innate knack for honing in on management ackamarackus. So, if a leader is not on board with cybersecurity, then staff will not be on board either. This is bad.

A company's workforce is usually the focal point of attack for cybercriminals trying to hack into an organization's computer network. A culture of cybersecurity—or the lack thereof—will determine whether a company's people are its greatest defense or its weakest link against a brutal cyberattack.

It is critical for C-suite leaders to establish a cybersecurity *tone at the top* by holding themselves to a high standard of cyber hygiene. When company leaders talk the talk and walk the walk, employees are more likely to do the same, and cybersecurity becomes woven into the fabric of the organization's culture.

Big-ticket cyber technology is great—as is funding the cybersecurity program and hiring a top-notch CISO—but a cybercriminal only needs to trick one person into giving up a username and password, and down goes the network. A company's people can be an insurmountable bulwark against a cyberattack, or an all-access pass for cybercriminals to install malware.

Still, there is more to engaged oversight than supporting the CISO and establishing a tone at the top. C-suite leaders need to be fully accountable for the success or failure of the cybersecurity program. It's not enough to rely on the CIO and CISO; C-suite leaders need to have skin in the game.

But how can C-suite leaders truly *own* cybersecurity when it is such a highly technical field? C-suite leaders typically come from non-cyber backgrounds, such as finance or marketing, or from operational areas specific to the company's business, like clinical research in the pharmaceutical industry or design engineering in the automotive sector. Why should the C-suite take all the blame for a cyberattack when the company has a highly experienced CISO on board?

It's human nature to hand off what you don't know to a subject matter expert and rely on that person to get the job done. But C-suite leaders have a fiduciary duty to provide engaged oversight of the cybersecurity program. The best CISO on the planet cannot insulate C-suite leaders from personal liability, nor will a CISO be able to deflect the public outrage following a massive data breach or a cyberattack causing physical damage.

However, leadership accountability for cybersecurity does not mean C-suite leaders must have a technology background or be experts in cybersecurity. Accountability means C-suite leaders must have sufficient cybersecurity knowledge so that they can ensure the existence of an effective cybersecurity program. At a minimum, C-suite leaders must have a thorough understanding of *good cyber hygiene* (e.g., use strong passwords, turn on MFA, install patches, encrypt data, implement data backups, and launch workforce cybersecurity training). The C-suite should also have an understanding of the common *attack vectors* that cybercriminals use to launch devastating cyberattacks (e.g., weak or reused passwords, unpatched software vulnerabilities, phishing and other social engineering scams, etc.). The term I use to describe these two components of cybersecurity knowledge is *cyber-savvy*.

Knowledge isn't just power in the age of ransomware; it's eight USB drives lashed together like a bundle of dynamite primed to explode with a fuse lit by phishing attacks, reused passwords, and zero-day malware. To meet the challenge posed by bomb-throwing cybercriminals, C-suite leaders must be armed with a hefty amount of cyber-savvy to inspire the company to take on the bad guys. Cyber-savvy is also crucial in helping C-suite leaders fortify the company with the tools, policies, and programs necessary to defend against a destructive cyberattack.

A Cyber-Savvy C-Suite Is a Force to Be Reckoned With

You may have noticed I've not singled out the CISO as being solely accountable for cybersecurity, nor have I laid sole responsibility on the CIO, the information technology department, or the cybersecurity team. I have also not pointed my finger at the CEO as single-handedly blame-worthy for cybersecurity lapses.

Sure, there are a few high-profile cases where a devastating ransomware cyberattack led to the CEO, CIO, or CISO being shown the door. However, *cybersecurity is the shared responsibility of the entire senior leadership team*, not just a few executives at the top of the hierarchy. Cybersecurity is *owned* by the C-suite leadership team because no other group of leaders has the political and moral clout to ensure company systems are protected by an effective cybersecurity program deployed throughout the organization.

Two significant barriers to C-suite leaders discharging their role as cybersecurity champions are the highly technical nature of cybersecurity coupled with the ingenuity and technical sophistication of cybercriminals. It would not be fair to expect that C-suite leaders must come from information technology backgrounds or develop deep expertise in cybersecurity. However, to provide engaged oversight of the cybersecurity program, C-suite leaders must have a thorough understanding of good cyber hygiene principles. C-suite leaders must also understand the mindset of cybercriminals and the attack vectors they exploit to launch damaging cyberattacks. In short, C-suite leaders must be cyber-savvy.

Like heavyweight boxer Mike Tyson in his prime, a cyber-savvy C-suite is a force to be reckoned with—fierce, ripped, and itching to clobber the living daylights out of cybercriminals. But being cyber-savvy is more than paying lip service with an underfunded, bare-bones cybersecurity program that leaves your company with a fat lip from a ransomware sucker punch. C-suite leaders must step into the ring, bobbing and weaving with cyber hygiene awareness training, jabbing with strong passwords, and counter punching with multifactor authentication. Don't leave cybercriminals hanging on the ropes, waiting to be saved by the bell—knock them to the canvas and down for the count with a jaw-breaking cyber hygiene haymaker. C-suite leaders should not be satisfied merely going the distance with cybercriminals; it's time to get in the ring, put up a fight, knock out the bad guys, and be your company's cybersecurity champions.

It's the Passwords and the Patches, Stupid!

Democratic strategist James Carville coined the phrase, "It's the economy, stupid!" to galvanize Arkansas Governor Bill Clinton's successful run for president in 1992. But we can concoct a similar phrase for cybersecurity—*It's the passwords and the patches, stupid!*—to remind C-suite leaders that compromised passwords and unpatched software vulnerabilities are the cybercriminal's greatest opportunity and the company's greatest weakness.

Cybercriminals are obsessed with passwords and the C-suite should be as well. Passwords can be stolen by a phishing attack or purchased on the Dark Web, and weak passwords can be cracked by cybercriminals using brute force attack methodologies. Once a password is in the hands of a cybercriminal, it can be used to access a computer network and deliver a ransomware payload. Compromised passwords are the most common cause of successful cyberattacks, so C-suite leaders must have a fortress-like mentality around password management.

Software vulnerabilities are another passion of cybercriminals, who hunt for software coding errors like a pack of ravenous wolves. When a coding error is ferreted out by cybercriminals, the vulnerability can be exploited in a zero-day attack. That's why patch management is one of the most elemental countermeasures to avoiding a brutal ransomware attack.

It's up to the software vendor to flag the vulnerability before the bad guys and create a patch to correct the problem. The vendor will then issue the patch for installation by its customers—and now the race is on! Companies win the race by installing the patch before cybercriminals can launch the exploit; on the other hand, cybercriminals slap each other a *high-five!* when exploits penetrate the network because a corrective patch was not installed.

So there you have it—cybercriminals focus on the basics of hacking by stealing passwords or exploiting software vulnerabilities. Companies become victims by failing to build defenses around login credentials or by not installing patches in a timely manner. In other words, cybercriminals win when companies don't cover the basics of cybersecurity.

Basic countermeasures are the foundation of a cybersecurity program:

- Circle your wagons around the password! Weak passwords are easily cracked using brute force attacks, while reused passwords can be found on the Dark Web (from breaches at other organizations). Compromised passwords are the lifeblood of cybercriminals, so a password management policy mandating the use of strong passwords and prohibiting reused passwords is essential.

- Everyone makes mistakes, and sometimes an employee will be tricked by a phishing scam and give up their username and password. As an extra layer of security, MFA should be enabled across the enterprise. MFA requires the use of a one-time numeric code, in addition to the employee's login credentials, in order to access the network. If a cybercriminal has stolen a username and password but does not have the MFA numeric code, then the cybercriminal cannot gain access to the network.

- An organization is only one stolen password away from a cyberattack. It is incumbent upon companies to leverage the entire workforce to defend against ransomware and prevent massive data breaches. A phishing awareness training program is a call to arms for all employees to guard against social engineering trickery by cunning cybercriminals. A company's employees can be a mighty shield against ransomware or the chink in the armor that allows cybercriminals to pierce the network.

- Companies, vendors, and cybercriminals are in a race against time. Cybercriminals are sprinting toward a company's network brandishing the latest vulnerability exploit to inject a nasty ransomware payload and encrypt company data. Vendors are rushing to develop the corrective code that fixes the error and then scramble to publish the vector-shielding patch that will block the exploit. All the company needs to do is install the darn patch!

It is axiomatic that cybercriminals focus on the basics of hacking; therefore, companies must focus on the basics of cybersecurity. This means defending the company's network with a password management policy backed up by MFA and a phishing awareness program.

Oh, and C-suite leaders please take note: install the darn patches!

Two Sides of the Same Coin

Two of the most underrated, underappreciated, and therefore unmanaged cybersecurity risks are shadow IT and data offshoring. They are difficult risks to get a handle on because they are at once omnipresent and invisible. In fact, shadow IT and data offshoring share some common characteristics:

- *Ubiquity*: Shadow IT and data offshoring are widespread practices in many companies.
- *Popularity*: Shadow IT is very popular with employees who believe a particular app or device conveys productivity benefits, even though the technology has not been approved by the company. Likewise, outsourcing functions to foreign-based vendors is a popular way to reduce costs and increase productivity. So, both shadow IT and data offshoring are seen by employees and management as providing substantial benefits to their work and the company as a whole.
- *Invisibility*: Shadow IT is very, very hard to identify because employees can easily obtain the latest app or device online and often for free (e.g., many apps have tiered pricing, starting with a cost of $0!). In a similar vein, data offshoring happens right under the noses of leaders because a vendor could be offshoring and not tell anyone.
- *Unappreciated risk*: Employees and management see the benefits of shadow IT and data offshoring; however, they generally

do not appreciate the tremendous cybersecurity risks these practices pose to the company.

You can see why it's so hard to get your arms around shadow IT and data offshoring. Nonetheless, the effort must be made as shadow IT and data offshoring are very risky practices, and if they are not dealt with, can lead to a ransomware cyberattack or a massive data breach (and probably both!).

The truth is many companies are up to their eyeballs in shadow IT and data offshoring and don't even know it. This means companies need to adopt policies to ferret out shadow IT and data offshoring, and once identified, go after the risks with dogged tenacity.

Small but Mighty (Dangerous)

Get a grip on your thumb drives! Small in stature but standing tall in storage, USB drives are the king of removable media. USB drives, CDs, and the like are popular means to store and access data when working at home or traveling on company business. But to cybercriminals, USB drives are a favorite hacking tool brimming with malware designed to steal data from your computer or deliver ransomware to your company's network.

Companies can lessen the risk by installing antivirus software that will scan the USB drive as soon as it's inserted into the computer's port. Encryption software should also be installed, so when a USB drive is lost or stolen, the data will not fall into the hands of cybercriminals.

Employees should be trained on the dangers of removable media; in particular, employees should be warned to never connect to an unknown device. Cybercriminals will drop USB drives and charging cables in public places hoping unsuspecting travelers insert them into a device, but all they get for their curiosity is a ransomware payload.

Traveling employees should never use public USB ports to charge their devices. Always use a company-issued charging cable and the tried-and-true wall outlet; this way, you get a good charge minus the malware.

Still, removable media is dinosaur technology best left to the stone age. Cloud storage and shared drives offer a convenient and *always available* storage format with the value-added benefit of far greater security.

Given the enormous risks posed by malware-stuffed USB drives—aka BadUSBs—organizations are wise to limit the use of USB drives by implementing an enterprisewide device control policy (DCP), enforced by device control software. Also, whitelisted devices should be configured with file sharing protocols to constrain the amount of data that can be packed onto a USB drive.

USB drives are outmoded and dangerous. Worse, in the hands of a cybercriminal, they are a ticking time bomb. Given the outsized risk, companies need to get a handle on USB drives before they go ... BOOM!

No Excuses Zone

Nothing in life is perfect, and when strong passwords and MFA let you down, encryption will be there to give you a big, warm hug. Encryption will be there for you when company employees are tricked into revealing passwords. Encryption will console you when that expensive-looking laptop gets stolen from the backseat of an employee's car. Encryption will even pour you a soothing cup of coffee when an employee forgets to wipe a server that was decommissioned. Alright, yeah. Encryption won't actually pour you a coffee, but it just might save your bacon when a cyber disaster strikes.

Encryption is the last line of defense when data is lost or stolen; if it's encrypted, then the bad guys can't get it. When companies encrypt their data, cyberattacks are foiled, breaches are denied, and the bad guys lose. Most importantly, innocent people whose data was lost will not be hurt when the data is encrypted and not accessible by cybercriminals.

To put it bluntly, there is no excuse for not encrypting data, and companies that lose unencrypted data should expect to pay harsh fines and penalties.

Don't Go Down With the Ship

When the microchips are down, data backup has your back, and that's no bull. It's not a sexy technology like artificial intelligence or that whole blockchain craze, but when ransomware strikes, it's the power of data backup that turns the lights back on.

Data backups are the most unloved and underappreciated counter-measure in cybersecurity, but just because backing stuff up is akin to scraping the barnacles off a battleship, doesn't mean it's not worthy of respect.

Barnacles won't sink your boat, but they will slow it down to a crawl; ransomware, however, will sink your company to the bottom of the sea without data backup. So, if you own a boat, scrape the barnacles, and if you run a company, back up the data!

The Biggest Vector

Social media is, by a wide margin, the biggest attack vector in all of cyber-security. Monolithic and controversial, social media platforms simultane-ously spew wisdom and disinformation to billions of people in the blink of an eye.

Small wonder that cybercriminals and plain-vanilla con artists grav-itate to social media platforms to launch destructive cyberattacks on a massive scale. Brandjacking can sully a company's reputation and irre-trievably sever the connection between the company and its loyal base of customers. Disgruntled employees could bust open a spigot of corpo-rate innuendo and biased commentary redefining a company's standing with both its workforce and customers. Posting too much information on social media can lead to phishing cyberattacks and even crimes against individual employees.

Organizations must take a holistic approach to tamp down the risks of social media. This will take an *all hands on deck* mentality of engag-ing the entire workforce to be on alert for social media-borne scams and cyberattacks.

Organizations must ensure their social media accounts are secured with strong passwords that are never reused or shared by department staff. It is also critical to enable MFA for an extra layer of security. These countermeasures can prevent a cybercriminal from taking over a compa-ny's social media account, making brandjacking a hard sell right from the get-go.

It is also vital to monitor social media platforms for mentions and conversations about the company. Ferret out brandjacking with a social media listening tool so the company can respond quickly and effectively to limit damage to its brand and customer base. Finding out about false or negative information days after it's posted is inexcusable and will result in lasting damage.

Companies must develop a strategy to handle negative posts by disgruntled and former employees. That's why it's important to craft a social media policy in line with the laws of your home country. Managing employees and their posts raise a host of legal and ethical issues; worse, it can be quite awkward. A social media policy will be your roadmap to dealing with these thorny issues.

The social media policy should be communicated to your workforce along with a social media awareness program to alert your employees about the risks they face in using social media. Employees should be cautioned not to post too much information giving cybercriminals an edge in launching a cyberattack on the company or attempting to defraud individual employees. Simple things like not wearing the company badge in a photo or not sharing personal details in a post could prevent employees from becoming the victims of a cybercrime. Too much information is dangerous; cautious posting will help block cybercriminals from discovering vulnerabilities and avenues of attack.

Inspire a Culture of Cybersecurity Awareness

People, not technology, are an organization's greatest defense against a cyberattack. On the flip-side, when malware gums up the network and data breaches run wild, you can bet unsuspecting employees were the gateway to ransomware hell. The most effective countermeasure against cybercriminals and their bag of tricks is a companywide culture of cybersecurity. Employees that put cyber hygiene into practice are unbeatable.

That's why employee buy-in of cybersecurity best practices is critical in preventing the company from being that next ransomware statistic. To make cybersecurity engaging to employees, awareness programs should focus on the basics and be presented in a fun, non-geeky way. Employees do not need to be cybersecurity nerds! They just need to know the cybersecurity basics to prevent becoming the victim of a social engineering scam or inadvertently uploading a malware virus into the network.

The basics will set you free, and it doesn't get any more basic than telling your workforce to only login with strong passwords, never reuse or share them, and always use MFA when it is available.

You'd be surprised how many employees don't know about phishing scams—so tell them! Explain to them how cybercriminals attempt to trick them into clicking on a link in an e-mail that delivers malware. Or how cybercriminals will try and con them into giving up their username and password. A good phishing awareness program will provide examples of how this trickery occurs, along with illustrations of fake e-mails that employees should be wary of.

And don't just tell them, show them with your own internal phishing campaign, by sending employees fake e-mails that provide instant pop-up education when they click on the fake link and get phished.

Physical security is another core component of a cybersecurity awareness program. To avoid theft, employees should be warned to guard their devices at all times. This means locking up devices when they leave the work area, securing devices in the car trunk when traveling, and never leaving removable media (such as USB drives) laying around where they can be easily pilfered.

Employees should also be informed about the sneaky ways cybercriminals enter company property and scam their way into sensitive areas. Employees should be careful to make sure no one sneaks in behind them when badging in (known as tailgating), and they should be aware of cybercriminals pretending to be someone they are not (such as a building inspector) to gain access to a secure area (known as piggybacking).

Awareness programs should also tell employees to shred sensitive documents and not throw them in the trash, where a dumpster-diving criminal can nab them. Employees should also be warned that cybercriminals will litter the parking lot with USB drives containing malware, so employees should never plug in an unapproved USB drive into a company computer.

Traveling and work-from-home employees should be careful when they connect to a public Wi-Fi network. Cybercriminals can concoct fake Wi-Fi landing pages that look like a real coffee shop or hotel landing page and track everything the employee does while on the evil portal. That's why employees working remotely should always use the company VPN, which will encrypt the employee's work and keep everything private.

Fighting Back

Let's toss a coin and see what happens. If a cybercriminal calls *heads* but the coin flips *tails*, then the cybercriminal loses. But don't make the mistake of thinking the game is over. The coin can flip *tails* time and time again, but eventually, the coin flips *heads* and the cybercriminal wins. Cybercriminals have it easy. They can lose a million times, but one win is all it takes to launch a withering cyberattack. It's time for companies to opt-out of this losing paradigm and stop playing the cybercriminal's rigged game.

Freedom from cyber doom means focusing on the basics: password management, MFA, phishing awareness training for employees, and patching systems. Cyber hygiene is not optional; it is the cost of doing business in the age of ransomware.

Everyone makes mistakes, so it's vital to have a Plan B when Plan A blows up in your face. When a countermeasure fails, encrypting all devices will prevent stolen data from falling into the wrong hands. Likewise, if a cybercriminal bypasses a countermeasure to lock down a network, the company's data backup plan stands ready to restore operations.

Notice the use of the word *vital* in the preceding paragraph: Plan B is not optional!

C-suite leaders also need a healthy appreciation for unseen risks. Shadow IT, data offshoring, mobile devices, and social media are fertile breeding grounds for cybercriminals and alluring targets for cyberattacks.

Most importantly, organizational culture is the key to warding off cyberattacks. Leadership accountability is fundamental to cybersecurity at a sub-atomic level. The top leaders and the board of trustees must own cybersecurity. Without tone at the top, there is no cybersecurity, and it is only a matter of when—and how bad—your business gets hacked.

C-suite leaders, you can do this. But more to the point: you MUST do this. C-suite leaders unquestionably face a daunting set of challenges in a world that seems like it's going to hell in a handbasket. Yet despite a global pandemic, broken supply chains, and recession fears, millions of heroes stand tall, performing their jobs with a superhuman, selfless dedication to their customers, co-workers, and communities. C-suite leaders can be no less dedicated to providing the highest level of cybersecurity and data protection possible.

References

Preface

Babinski, M. November 22, 2021. "Why the 'Basement Hacker' Stereotype Is Wrong—and Dangerous." *Dark Reading.* www.darkreading.com/attacks-breaches/why-the-basement-hacker-stereotype-is-wrong-and-dangerous (accessed August 02, 2022).

Baker, K. February 07, 2022. "Ransomware as a Service (RaaS) Explained. *CrowdStrike.* https://www.crowdstrike.com/cybersecurity-101/ransomware/ransomware-as-a-service-raas/ (accessed January 12, 2023).

Cranston, M. July 16, 2021. "What Scares Powell Most Is Not Inflation or China." *Australian Financial Review.* www.afr.com/policy/economy/what-scares-powell-most-is-not-inflation-or-china-20210716-p58a90 (accessed August 03, 2022).

Dice Staff. February 10, 2020. "How Cybercriminals Recruit and Look for Skilled Developers." *Dice Insights.* https://www.dice.com/career-advice/how-cybercriminals-recruit-skilled-developers (accessed January 11, 2023).

Irei, A. January 24, 2022. "What Is Cyber Hygiene and Why Is It Important?" *TechTarget.* www.techtarget.com/searchsecurity/definition/cyber-hygiene (accessed December 16, 2022).

McKeon, J. May 05, 2022. "Best Practices for Password Security, Cyber Hygiene." *HealthITSecurity.* https://healthitsecurity.com/news/best-practices-for-password-security-cyber-hygiene (accessed December 16, 2022).

Ritesh, K. March 13, 2021. "Who's Buying And Selling Ransomware Kits On the Dark Web." *Cybercrime Magazine.* https://cybersecurityventures.com/whos-buying-and-selling-ransomware-kits-on-the-dark-web/#:~:text=Prices%20for%20RaaS%20kits%20vary%20wildly%20depending%20on,some%20that%20cost%20tens%20of%20thousands%20of%20dollars (accessed January 11, 2023).

Son, H. April 04, 2019. "JP Morgan CEO Jamie Dimon Warns Cyberattacks 'Biggest Threat' to US." *CNBC.* www.cnbc.com/2019/04/04/jp-morgan-ceo-jamie-dimon-warns-cyber-attacks-biggest-threat-to-us.html (accessed August 03, 2022).

Van de Wiele, T. September 23, 2022. "We Need to Smash the Stereotype That Hackers are All Teens in Hoodies." *Silicon Republic.* www.siliconrepublic.com/enterprise/ethical-hacker-stereotype (accessed December 16, 2022).

Whitney, L. October 13, 2021. "Dark Web: Many Cybercrime Services Sell for Less than $500." *TechRepublic.* https://www.techrepublic.com/article/dark-web-many-cybercrime-services-sell-for-less-than-500/#:~:text=A%20ransom ware%20kit%20costs%20as%20little%20as%20%2466%2C,ransom ware%2C%20phishing%20campaigns%2C%20and%20other%20 types%20of%20attacks (accessed January 11, 2023).

Chapter 1

Bunge, J. June 09, 2021. "JBS Paid $11 Million to Resolve Ransomware Attack." *Wall Street Journal.* www.wsj.com/articles/jbs-paid-11-million-to-resolve-ransomware-attack-11623280781 (accessed August 09, 2022).

Burgess, M. March 07, 2017. "What Is the Petya Ransomware Spreading across Europe? WIRED Explains." *WIRED UK.* www.wired.co.uk/article/ petya-malware-ransomware-attack-outbreak-june-2017 (accessed August 18, 2022).

Cerulus, L. February 14, 2019. "How Ukraine Became a Test Bed for Cyberweaponry." *POLITICO.* www.politico.eu/article/ukraine-cyber-war-frontline-russia-malware-attacks/ (accessed August 18, 2022).

Cisco. February 25, 2021. "Oldsmar's Cyber Attack Raises the Alarm for the Water Industry." *GovTech.* www.govtech.com/sponsored/oldsmars-cyber-attack-raises-the-alarm-for-the-water-industry.html (accessed August 19, 2022).

Cybersecurity and Infrastructure Security Agency. November 22, 2021. "CISA and FBI Urge Organizations to Remain Vigilant to Ransomware and Cyber Threats This Holiday Season." www.cisa.gov/news/2021/11/22/cisa-and-fbi-urge-organizations-remain-vigilant-ransomware-and-cyber-threats.

Kipling, R. 1889. "The Ballad of East and West." *Public Domain Poetry.* www .public-domain-poetry.com/rudyard-kipling/ballad-of-east-and-west-3111 (accessed August 25, 2022).

McKay, T. December 10, 2021. "Ransomware Jerks Helped Cause the Cream Cheese Shortage." *Gizmodo.* https://gizmodo.com/ransomware-jerks-helped-cause-the-cream-cheese-shortage-1848195368 (accessed August 09, 2022).

Morrison, S. June 08, 2021. "The Colonial Pipeline Ransomware Cyberattack: How a Major Oil Pipeline Got Held for Ransom." *Vox.* www.vox.com/ recode/22428774/ransomeware-pipeline-colonial-darkside-gas-prices (accessed August 15, 2022).

Parsons, L. March 21, 2021. "Chinese Cyberattack Almost Shut off Power for Three Million Australians." *Daily Mail Online.* www.dailymail.co.uk/ news/article-10283839/Chinese-cyberattack-shut-power-three-million-Australians.html (accessed August 19, 2022).

Shepel, J. October 28, 2021. "Schreiber Foods Hit With Cyberattack; Plants Closed." *Wisconsin State Farmer.* www.wisfarmer.com/story/news/2021/10/26/

schreiber-foods-hit-cyberattack-plants-closed/8558252002/ (accessed August 09, 2022).

Smith, C. April 13, 2022. "What Is the Dark Web & How to Get There?" KnowTechie. https://knowtechie.com/what-is-the-dark-web-how-to-get-there/ (accessed August 12, 2022).

Turton, W. and K. Mehrotra. June 04, 2021. "Hackers Breached Colonial Pipeline Using Compromised Password." *Bloomberg.* www.bloomberg.com/news/articles/2021-06-04/hackers-breached-colonial-pipeline-using-compromised-password (accessed August 16, 2022).

U.S. Food and Drug Administration. October 01, 2019. "FDA Informs Patients, Providers and Manufacturers about Potential Cybersecurity Vulnerabilities for Connected Medical Devices and Health Care Networks That Use Certain Communication Software." www.fda.gov/news-events/press-announcements/fda-informs-patients-providers-and-manufacturers-about-potential-cybersecurity-vulnerabilities.

Zetter, K. November 03, 2014. "An Unprecedented Look at Stuxnet, the World's First Digital Weapon." *Wired.* www.wired.com/2014/11/countdown-to-zero-day-stuxnet/ (accessed August 22, 2022).

Chapter 2

Barrett, B. August 19, 2018. "How to Protect Your Phone Against a SIM Swap Attack." *Wired.* www.wired.com/story/sim-swap-attack-defend-phone/ (accessed August 30, 2022).

Cimpanu, C. October 07, 2019. "FBI Warns About Attacks That Bypass Multi-Factor Authentication (MFA)." *ZDNet.* www.zdnet.com/article/fbi-warns-about-attacks-that-bypass-multi-factor-authentication-mfa/ (accessed August 31, 2022).

Cybersecurity & Infrastructure Security Agency. January, 2022. "Multi-Factor Authentication." www.cisa.gov/sites/default/files/publications/MFA-Fact-Sheet-Jan22-508.pdf.

Gatlan, S. February 09, 2022. "FBI Warns of Criminals Escalating SIM Swap Attacks to Steal Millions." *BleepingComputer.* https://www.bleepingcomputer.com/news/security/fbi-warns-of-criminals-escalating-sim-swap-attacks-to-steal-millions/ (accessed January 12, 2023).

LMG Security. February 22, 2022. "New Phishing-as-a-Service Kits Bypass MFA—Here's What to Do Next." *LMG Security.* www.lmgsecurity.com/new-phishing-as-a-service-kits-bypass-mfa-heres-what-to-do-next/ (accessed August 31, 2022).

Montalbano, E. June 09, 2021. "DarkSide Pwned Colonial With Old VPN Password." *Threatpost.* https://threatpost.com/darkside-pwned-colonial-with-old-vpn-password/166743/ (accessed August 29, 2022).

Novinson, M. June 05, 2021. "Colonial Pipeline Hacked Via Inactive Account Without MFA." *CRN*. www.crn.com/news/security/colonial-pipeline-hacked-via-inactive-account-without-mfa (accessed August 29, 2022).

Rafter, D. August 15, 2022. "SIM Swap Fraud Explained and How to Help Protect Yourself." *Norton*. https://us.norton.com/blog/mobile/sim-swap-fraud# (accessed January 12, 2023).

Smith, J.A.. June 06, 2021. "Lack of Multi-Factor Authentication Caused Colonial Pipeline Breach." *Chattanoogan.Com*. www.chattanoogan.com/2021/6/6/429493/John-Anthony-Smith-Lack-Of.aspx (accessed August 29, 2022).

Trend Micro. February 23, 2022. "What Is a SIM Swap Scam & How to Stay Protected?" *Trend Micro News*. news.trendmicro.com/2022/02/23/what-is-a-sim-swap-scam-how-to-stay-protected/ (accessed August 30, 2022).

Winters, M. February 19, 2022. "How to Avoid SIM Card Scam That Once Fooled Jack Dorsey." *CNBC*. www.cnbc.com/2022/02/19/how-to-avoid-sim-card-scam-that-once-fooled-jack-dorsey.html (accessed August 30, 2022).

Chapter 3

AP News Bureau. December 02, 2022. "User Details Exposed After LastPass Suffered Major Data Breach." *ABP News LIVE*. https://news.abplive.com/technology/lastpass-password-manager-suffers-2nd-data-breach-in-2022-know-everything-1567072 (accessed December 23, 2022).

Cimpanu, C. September 27, 2019. "Dunkin' Donuts Says There's 'No Basis' for Lawsuit Over 2015 Security Incident." *ZDNet*. www.zdnet.com/article/dunkin-donuts-says-theres-no-basis-for-lawsuit-over-2015-security-incident/ (accessed September 07, 2022).

Clark, M. December 23, 2022. "Hackers Stole Encrypted LastPass Password Vaults, and We're Just Now Hearing about It." *The Verge*. www.theverge.com/2022/12/22/23523322/lastpass-data-breach-cloud-encrypted-password-vault-hackers (accessed December 23, 2022).

Cluley, G. September 17, 2020. "The Dunkin' Donuts Data Breach Leaves a Very Bad Taste in the Mouth." *Graham Cluley*. https://grahamcluley.com/the-dunkin-donuts-data-breach-leaves-a-very-bad-taste-in-the-mouth/ (accessed December 16, 2022).

Duong, J. April 28, 2022. "Password Manager KeePass Review: Robust Offline Alternative." *Locker*. https://locker.io/blog/password-manager-keepass-review (accessed January 06, 2023).

Heinzman, A. December 22, 2022. "The LastPass Data Breach Just Got Even Worse … Again." *Review Geek*. https://www.reviewgeek.com/140432/the-lastpass-data-breach-just-got-even-worse-again/ (accessed December 23, 2022).

James, D. November 26, 2021. "The Password Turns 60 This Year, But It's Not Going Away Anytime Soon." *Infosecurity Magazine*. www.infosecurity-magazine.com/opinions/password-turns-60-this-year/ (accessed December 19, 2022).

Kalat, D. November 04, 2018. "The History of Passwords and the Case of the First Theft." *ThinkSet*. https://thinksetmag.com/issue-6/the-case-of-the-purloined-password (accessed December 19, 2022).

Kan, M. January 05, 2023. "LastPass Faces Class-Action Lawsuit Over Password Vault Breach." *PCMag*. https://www.pcmag.com/news/lastpass-faces-class-action-lawsuit-over-password-vault-breach (accessed January 09, 2023).

New York State Attorney General. September 26, 2019. "Press Release: AG James Sues Dunkin' Donuts For Glazing Over Cyberattacks Targeting Thousands." https://ag.ny.gov/press-release/2019/ag-james-sues-dunkin-donuts-glazing-over-cyberattacks-targeting-thousands.

New York State Attorney General. September, 15 2020. "Press Release: Attorney General James Gets Dunkin' to Fill Holes in Security, Reimburse Hacked Customers." https://ag.ny.gov/press-release/2020/attorney-general-james-gets-dunkin-fill-holes-security-reimburse-hacked-customers.

Nichols, S. September 15, 2020. "Dunkin' Donuts Drops Some Dough to Glaze Over Lawsuit Accusing It of Covering Up Customer Account Hacks." *The Register*. www.theregister.com/2020/09/15/dunkin_donuts_cooks_up_deal/ (accessed December 16, 2022).

Ovide, S. January 10, 2023. "Four Realistic Steps to Upgrade Your Online Security." *The Washington Post*. https://www.washingtonpost.com/technology/2023/01/10/lastpass-breach-kill-passwords/ (accessed January 10, 2023).

Paez, D. March 17, 2020. "How "Pwned" Went From Hacker Slang to the Internet's Favorite Taunt." *Inverse*. www.inverse.com/gaming/pwned-meaning-definition-origins-video-games-internet-hackers (accessed December 14, 2022).

Summerson, C. July 23, 2020. "I Switched from LastPass to 1Password (and You Should, Too)." *Review Geek*. www.reviewgeek.com/47843/i-switched-from-lastpass-to-1password-and-you-should-too/ (accessed December 23, 2022).

Sze, M. September 18, 2020. "Dunkin' Donuts Agrees to Settle Over 5-Year-Old Data Breach—Myce.Com." *Myce.Com*. www.myce.com/news/dunkin-donuts-agrees-to-settle-over-5-year-old-data-breach-94431/ (accessed September 07, 2022).

The People of the State of New York, by Letitia James. September 26, 2019. Attorney General of the State of New York vs Dunkin' Brands, Inc. No. 451787/2019. Supreme Court of the State of New York. https://ag.ny.gov/sites/default/files/dunkin_complaint.pdf.

The People of the State of New York, by Letitia James. September 22, 2020. Attorney General of the State of New York vs Dunkin' Brands, Inc.

No. 451787/2019. Supreme Court of the State of New York. https://ag.ny.gov/sites/default/files/consent_order_so_ordered_final.pdf.

Toubba, K. December 22, 2022. "Notice of Recent Security Incident" *The LastPass Blog*. https://blog.lastpass.com/2022/12/notice-of-recent-security-incident/ (accessed December 23, 2022).

Yee, A. January 05, 2023. "LastPass Hacked: How to Export and Protect Your Passwords." *PCWorld*. https://www.pcworld.com/article/1445758/how-to-export-your-passwords-and-ditch-lastpass.html (accessed January 09, 2023).

Chapter 4

Farberov, S. March 16, 2021. "Florida Teen 'Mastermind' of Global Twitter Hack Agrees to Three-Year Prison Plea Deal." *Daily Mail Online*. www.dailymail.co.uk/news/article-9369033/Florida-teen-mastermind-global-Twitter-hack-agrees-three-year-prison-plea-deal.html (accessed September 12, 2022).

Francisco, E. July 15, 2020. "July 15 Twitter Hack: A List of Every Hacked Verified Account." *Inverse*. www.inverse.com/culture/a-complete-list-of-every-twitter-account-hacked-on-july-15 (accessed September 14, 2022).

George, D. October 22, 2020. "New York Department of Financial Services Releases Report on Twitter Hack." *The National Law Review*. www.natlawreview.com/article/new-york-department-financial-services-issues-report-recent-twitter-hack (accessed September 15, 2022).

New York Department of Financial Services. 2020. *Twitter Investigation Report*. www.dfs.ny.gov/Twitter_Report.

Rodriguez, S. July 31, 2020. "Twitter Hack: 17-Year-Old Accused of Masterminding Bitcoin Scam." *CNBC*. www.cnbc.com/2020/07/31/twitter-bitcoin-scam-masterminded-by-17-year-old.html (accessed September 12, 2022).

Violino, B. January 07, 2023. "Phishing Attacks Are Increasing and Getting More Sophisticated." *CNBC*. https://www.cnbc.com/2023/01/07/phishing-attacks-are-increasing-and-getting-more-sophisticated.html (accessed January 07, 2023).

Whittaker, Z. September 30, 2020, "After Breach, Twitter Hires a New Cybersecurity Chief." *TechCrunch*. https://techcrunch.com/2020/09/30/twitter-ciso-rinki-sethi/ (accessed September 15, 2022).

Wilson, J. August 25, 2022. "What Is Vishing, And Why Is It A Threat." *Forbes*. https://www.forbes.com/advisor/personal-finance/what-is-vishing/ (accessed January 12, 2023).

Zorz, Z. July 31, 2020. "Twitter Employees Were Spear-Phished over the Phone." *Help Net Security*. www.helpnetsecurity.com/2020/07/31/twitter-employees-spear-phished/ (accessed September 12, 2022).

Chapter 5

AuditBoard. September 24, 2021. "NIST Password Guidelines: The New Requirements You Need to Know." *AuditBoard.* www.auditboard.com/blog/nist-password-guidelines/#:~:text=NIST%20requires%20an%208%2Dcharacter%20minimum%20for%20passwords (accessed September 20, 2022).

Fruhlinger, J. May 17, 2022. "Keyloggers Explained: How Attackers Record Computer Inputs | CSO Online." *CSO Online.* CSO. www.csoonline.com/article/3326304/keyloggers-explained-how-attackers-record-computer-inputs.html (accessed September 21, 2022).

Leonardo, L. June 02, 2021. "Fake Android Apps Use Imitation to Spread Malware: What You Need To Know." *ScreenRant.* https://screenrant.com/popular-fake-android-apps-imitated-malware-spread-explained/ (accessed September 21, 2022).

RSI Security. October 14, 2020. "Why You Need a Password Management Policy." *RSI Security.* https://blog.rsisecurity.com/why-you-need-a-password-management-policy/ (accessed September 20, 2022).

Smith, D.A. July 11, 2019. "Top 15 Password Management Best Practices." *BeyondTrust.* www.beyondtrust.com/blog/entry/top-15-password-management-best-practices (accessed September 20, 2022).

WP SitePlan. September 10, 2019. "What Are Brute Force Attacks and How to Prevent Them?" *WP SitePlan.* https://wpsiteplan.com/blog/what-are-brute-force-attacks/(accessed September 21, 2022).

Chapter 6

Dice Staff. May 12, 2022. "Bug Bounty Hunters: From Side Hustle to Tech Career." *Dice Insights.* https://www.dice.com/career-advice/bug-bounty-hunters-from-side-hustle-to-tech-career (accessed January 12, 2023).

Fruhlinger, J. August 24, 2022. "WannaCry Explained: A Perfect Ransomware Storm." *CSO Online.* www.csoonline.com/article/3227906/what-is-wannacry-ransomware-how-does-it-infect-and-who-was-responsible.html (accessed December 12, 2022).

Katz, Y. December 24, 2010. "Stuxnet May Have Destroyed 1,000 Centrifuges at Natanz." *The Jerusalem Post.* www.jpost.com/Defense/Stuxnet-may-have-destroyed-1000-centrifuges-at-Natanz (accessed September 27, 2022).

Leyden, J. October 20, 2016. "US DNC Hackers Blew through SIX Zero-Days Vulns Last Year Alone." *The Register.* www.theregister.com/2016/10/20/alleged_dnc_hackers_six_zerodays/ (accessed September 26, 2022).

Nakashima, E. and S. Harris. July 13, 2018. "How the Russians Hacked the DNC and Passed Its Emails to WikiLeaks." *The Washington Post.* www

.washingtonpost.com/world/national-security/how-the-russians-hacked-the-dnc-and-passed-its-emails-to-wikileaks/2018/07/13/af19a828-86c3-11e8-8553-a3ce89036c78_story.html (accessed September 26, 2022).

Noone, G. December 02, 2021. "The rise and rise of bug bounty hunting." *TechMonitor*. https://techmonitor.ai/technology/cybersecurity/rise-and-rise-of-bug-bounty-hunting (accessed January 12, 2023).

Palmer, D. August 03, 2017. "WannaCry Ransomware: Hackers Behind Global Cyberattack Finally Cash out Bitcoin Windfall." *ZDNet*. www.zdnet.com/article/wannacry-ransomware-hackers-behind-global-cyberattack-finally-cash-out-bitcoin-windfall/ (accessed September 24, 2022).

Perlroth, N. May 29, 2021. "The D.N.C. Didn't Get Hacked in 2020. Here's Why." *The New York Times*. www.nytimes.com/2021/05/29/us/politics/democratic-national-committee-hack.html (accessed September 26, 2022).

SentinelOne. May 27, 2019. "EternalBlue Exploit: What It Is And How It Works." *SentinelOne*. www.sentinelone.com/blog/eternalblue-nsa-developed-exploit-just-wont-die/ (accessed September 24, 2022).

Wattles, J. and J. Disis. May 15, 2017. "Ransomware Attack: Who's Been Hit." *CNNMoney*. https://money.cnn.com/2017/05/15/technology/ransomware-whos-been-hit/ (accessed September 23, 2022).

Chapter 7

House Oversight and Reform Committee. November 16, 2021. *Supplemental Memo on Committee's Investigation into Ransomware*. https://docs.house.gov/meetings/GO/GO00/20211116/114235/HHRG-117-GO00-20211116-SD005.pdf.

Miller, M. November 16, 2021. "Oversight Finds 'Small Lapses' in Security Led to Colonial Pipeline, JBS Hacks." *The Hill*. https://thehill.com/policy/cybersecurity/581800-house-oversight-panel-finds-that-small-lapses-in-security-led-to-recent/ (accessed September 29, 2022).

Schwirtz, M. May 14, 2021. "DarkSide, Blamed for Colonial Pipeline Attack, Says It Is Shutting Down." *The New York Times*. www.nytimes.com/2021/05/14/business/darkside-pipeline-hack.html (accessed September 29, 2022).

Chapter 8

Candia, T. March 22, 2021. "How to Proactively Manage Shadow IT." *EdTech*. https://edtechmagazine.com/higher/article/2021/03/how-proactively-manage-shadow-it (accessed December 16, 2022).

Greenlee, M. July 07, 2022. "How to Solve for Shadow IT in Your Organization." *Security Intelligence*. https://securityintelligence.com/articles/how-to-fix-shadow-it/ (accessed December 16, 2022).

Kirvan, P. October 07, 2021. "6 Dangers of Shadow IT and How to Avoid Them." *SearchCIO*. www.techtarget.com/searchcio/tip/6-dangers-of-shadow-IT-and-how-to-avoid-them (accessed December 16, 2022).

Shacklett, M. April 16, 2018. "5 Tips for Managing Shadow IT Without Destroying Innovation." *TechRepublic*. www.techrepublic.com/article/5-tips-for-managing-shadow-it-without-destroying-innovation/#:~:text=5%20 tips%20for%20managing%20shadow%20IT%20without%20 destroying,...%205%205.%20Accept%20vendor%20management%20 responsibilities%20 (accessed December 16, 2022).

Chapter 9

Baca, A. and R. Mendrez. March 26, 2020. "Would You Exchange Your Security for a Gift Card?" *Trustwave*. www.trustwave.com/en-us/resources/blogs/spiderlabs-blog/would-you-exchange-your-security-for-a-gift-card/ (accessed October 06, 2022).

Bisson, D. September 09, 2016. "Shocking! USB Killer Uses Electrical Charge to Fry Vulnerable Devices." *BleepingComputer*. www.bleepingcomputer.com/news/security/shocking-usb-killer-uses-electrical-charge-to-fry-vulnerable-devices/ (accessed October 04, 2022).

Cirelly, J. September 21, 2021. "BadUSB—What Is It and How to Avoid It in 2022 Step-by-Step Guide." *Comparitech*. www.comparitech.com/net-admin/what-is-badusb/ (accessed October 05, 2022).

Hamm, C. November 29, 2019. "Those Free, Innocent-Looking USB Charging Ports Could Rob You Blind." *Los Angeles Times*. www.latimes.com/travel/story/2019-11-29/juice-jacking-usb-charging-port (accessed October 04, 2022).

Hill, M. January 20, 2022. "BadUSB Explained: How Rogue USBs Threaten Your Organization | CSO Online." *CSO Online*. CSO. www.csoonline.com/article/3647173/badusb-explained-how-rogue-usbs-threaten-your-organization.html (accessed October 05, 2022).

Chapter 10

Banerjee, I., B. Sudhir, and P. Thakur. February, 2008. "Security Framework and Best Practices in Offshore Outsourcing." *Technology Partners International, Inc.* https://itonews.eu/files/f1213012284.pdf (accessed January 31, 2023).

Banerjee, S. April 06, 2016. "Is Outsourcing and/or Offshoring a Potential Threat to Cyber Security?" *LinkedIn*. www.linkedin.com/pulse/outsourcing-andor-offshoring-potential-threat-cyber-supantha-banerjee (accessed October 11, 2022).

Brisken, A., L. Earl, G. Hinkley, and J. E. Kendall. October, 2014. "Offshoring Health Information: Issues and Lingering Concerns." *Journal of Health &*

Life Sciences Law. https://sharepoint.healthlawyers.org/find-a-resource/Health
LawHub/Documents/Cybersecurity/Journal_2014_Offshoring%20Health
%20Information.pdf (accessed January 31, 2023).

Gupta, A. April 16, 2020. "5 Data Security Precautions to Take While Working
with Offshore Teams." *Colocation America*. https://www.colocationamerica
.com/blog/data-security-with-offshore-teams (accessed January 31, 2023).

Heaphy, M., and T. Simonis. December 01, 2022. "Outsourcing: United States
Overview." *Wiggin and Dana LLP*. https://content.next.westlaw.com/practical-
law/document/I2ef128e01ed511e38578f7ccc38dcbee/Outsourcing-United-
States-Overview?viewType=FullText&ppcid=a5d4ccb8124843f5a94c630
5ecc6e652&originationContext=knowHow&transitionType=KnowHow
Item&contextData=(sc.Default)&firstPage=true (accessed January 30, 2023).

Jackson, E. May 31, 2019. "Offshoring Private Health Information." *Jackson
LLP Healthcare Lawyers*. https://jacksonllp.com/offshoring-private-health-
information/ (accessed December 16, 2022).

Mahn, A. October 23, 2018. "Identify, Protect, Detect, Respond and Recover:
The NIST Cybersecurity Framework." *National Institute of Standards and
Technology*. www.nist.gov/blogs/taking-measure/identify-protect-detect-respond-
and-recover-nist-cybersecurity-framework (accessed October 13, 2022).

McGee, M. K. December 10, 2017. "Offshoring PHI: Addressing the Security
Issues." *Information Security Media Group*. https://www.careersinfosecurity
.com/offshoring-phi-addressing-security-issues-a-10530 (accessed January 30,
2023).

Nash, B., M. DeLancey, C. Allen, and A. Lack. July 21, 2014. "United States:
State False Claims Act Analysis: Does Your State Contract Prohibit Offshore
Outsourcing?" *Blank Rome*. https://www.mondaq.com/unitedstates/govern
ment-contracts-procurement-ppp/328562/state-false-claims-act-analysis-
does-your-state-contract-prohibit-offshore-outsourcing (accessed January 30,
2023).

Salazar, L. 2006. "Offshore Outsourcing: Protecting Privacy A World Away."
LawJournalNewsletters.Com. www.lawjournalnewsletters.com/sites/lawjournal
newsletters/2006/11/17/offshore-outsourcing-protecting-privacy-a-world-
away-2/?slreturn=20220318112505 (accessed October 13, 2022).

Vijayan, J. February 20, 2004. "Offshore Outsourcing Poses Privacy Perils."
Computerworld. www.computerworld.com/article/2574317/offshore-out
sourcing-poses-privacy-perils.html (accessed October 11, 2022).

Chapter 11

Bell, M. March 29, 2022. "List of GDPR Countries and Non-GDPR Countries
(Updated)." *SixFifty*. www.sixfifty.com/blog/gdpr-countries/ (accessed
October 19, 2022).

Department of Health and Human Services Office for Civil Rights. 2013. *HIPAA FAQs for Professionals: Is the Use of Encryption Mandatory in the Security Rule?* www.hhs.gov/hipaa/for-professionals/faq/2001/is-the-use-of-encryption-mandatory-in-the-security-rule/index.html.

Department of Health and Human Services. July 27, 2020. *Press Release: Lifespan Pays $1,040,000 to OCR to Settle Unencrypted Stolen Laptop Breach.* https://public3.pagefreezer.com/content/HHS.gov/31-12-2020T08:51/https://www.hhs.gov/about/news/2020/07/27/lifespan-pays-1040000-ocr-settle-unencrypted-stolen-laptop-breach.html.

The Fox Group. April 12, 2022. "HIPAA Encryption—Required or Not?" *The Fox Group Blog.* https://www.foxgrp.com/hipaa-encryption#:~:text=Technically%2C%20no%20HIPAA%20encryption%20is%20required.%20It%20is,health%20information.%20HIPAA%20data%20at%20rest%20%E2%80%9Cprotection%E2%80%9D%20requirements (accessed January 06, 2023).

Guez, Y. 2016. "6 Encryption Mistakes That Lead to Data Breaches." *Crypteron.* www.crypteron.com/blog/the-real-problem-with-encryption/ (accessed October 17, 2022).

HIPAA Journal. November 06, 2019. "Lack of Encryption Leads to $3 Million HIPAA Penalty for New York Medical Center." *HIPAA Journal.* www.hipaajournal.com/lack-of-encryption-leads-to-3-million-hipaa-penalty-for-new-york-medical-center/ (accessed October 18, 2022).

Lake, J. March 18, 2021. "What Is TLS Encryption and How Does It Work?" *Comparitech.* www.comparitech.com/blog/information-security/tls-encryption/ (accessed October 17, 2022).

Marks, L. April 08, 2020. "The California Consumer Privacy Act and Encryption." *ISACA.* www.isaca.org/resources/isaca-journal/issues/2020/volume-2/the-california-consumer-privacy-act-and-encryption (accessed October 18, 2022).

Reputation Mart. 2017. "How Will GDPR Impact Your Organization's Reputation." *Reputation Mart.* www.reputationmart.com/blog/how-will-gdpr-impact-your-organizations-online-reputation (accessed October 19, 2022).

Sunny Valley Networks. n.d. "What Is the Advanced Encryption Standard (AES)?" *Sunny Valley Networks.* www.sunnyvalley.io/docs/network-security-tutorials/what-is-advanced-encryption-standard-aes (accessed October 17, 2022).

Thomas, R. April 23, 2020. "Advanced Encryption Standard (AES): What It Is and How It Works." *Hashed Out by The SSL Store.* www.thesslstore.com/blog/advanced-encryption-standard-aes-what-it-is-and-how-it-works/ (accessed October 17, 2022).

Waksman, M. November 20, 2019. "Does GDPR Require Encryption?" *Jetico.* www.jetico.com/blog/does-gdpr-require-encryption (accessed October 19, 2022).

Chapter 12

Bonnette, C.A. January 12, 2004. "Business Continuity Planning—At the Top of 2004's 'To Do' List." *BankersOnline*. www.bankersonline.com/articles/106454 (accessed October 21, 2022).

Newsome, A. June 20, 2022. "Air gap Backups: What They Are and How They Work." *The Quest Blog*. https://blog.quest.com/what-is-an-air-gap-backup-is-it-necessary/ (accessed December 16, 2022).

Perot, T. January 10, 2019. "Adding an Air Gap to the 3-2-1 Backup Rule." *Global Data Vault*. www.globaldatavault.com/blog/air-gapped-backup-rule/ (accessed December 16, 2022).

Rouse, G. December 11, 2021. "Backup Strategy: What Is the 3-2-1 Backup Rule?" *Datto*. www.datto.com/blog/backup-strategy-what-is-the-3-2-1-backup-rule#:~:text=The%203%2D2%2D1%20backup%20rule%20states%20that%20you%20should,and%20is%20still%20relevant%20today (accessed October 21, 2022).

Chapter 13

Arici, A. April 01, 2022. "How to Set Up Two-Factor Authentication (2FA) on Various Social Networks." *Make Tech Easier*. https://www.maketecheasier.com/set-up-two-factor-authentication-social-networks/ (accessed January 08, 2023).

Burton, N. June 11, 2021. "When Does Sharing Become Oversharing?" *The Verge*. www.theverge.com/22526811/oversharing-social-media-protect-personal-harassment (accessed October 27, 2022).

Gaudin, S. August 19, 2015. "Target Troll Proves It's All or Nothing With Corporate Social Media." *Computerworld*. www.computerworld.com/article/2973513/target-troll-proves-it-s-all-or-nothing-with-corporate-social-media.html (accessed October 25, 2022).

Marketing Insider Group. January 29, 2018. "5 Ways to Protect Your Business Against Brandjacking." *Marketing Insider Group*. https://marketinginsidergroup.com/strategy/protect-business-brandjacking/ (accessed October 25, 2022).

National Labor Relations Board. 2022. "The NLRB and Social Media." *National Labor Relations Board*. www.nlrb.gov/about-nlrb/rights-we-protect/your-rights/the-nlrb-and-social-media (accessed October 25, 2022).

Nias, S. May 29, 2014. "Heinz Hit by Twitter 'brand-Jacking'." *PR Week*. www.prweek.com/article/1296428/heinz-hit-twitter-brand-jacking (accessed December 12, 2022).

Trend Micro. July 22, 2022. "Your Social Media Accounts Are at Risk of Being Hacked: Here's What to Do." *Trend Micro News*. https://news.trendmicro

.com/2022/07/22/two-factor-authentication-everything-you-need-to-know/ (accessed January 08, 2023).

The University of Chicago. 2017. "Smart Social Media." The University of Chicago. https://security.uchicago.edu/smart-social-media-2/ (accessed February 04, 2022).

Chapter 14

CISO MAG. December 30, 2019. "6 Practices to Strengthen Your Password Hygiene in 2020." *CISO MAG.* https://cisomag.eccouncil.org/6-practices-to-strengthen-your-password-hygiene-in-2020/ (accessed November 02, 2022).

Gendre, A. October 14, 2021. "Phishing Awareness Training: 8 Things Your Employees Should Understand." *Vade.* www.vadesecure.com/en/blog/phishing-awareness-training-8-things-employees-understand (accessed November 04, 2022).

Odogwu, C. November 23, 2022. "What Is an Evil Twin Attack and How Can You Prevent It?" *MUO.* www.makeuseof.com/what-is-evil-twin-attack/ (accessed November 29, 2022).

Packard, J. October 20, 2015. "How To Create a Cyber Secure Home." *Information Security UMass Lowell Blog.* https://blogs.uml.edu/information-security/2015/10/20/how-to-create-a-cyber-secure-home/ (accessed November 02, 2022).

Sanger, D.E. and J.E. Barnes. August 04, 2021. "Beware Free Wi-Fi: Government Urges Workers to Avoid Public Networks." *The New York Times.* www.nytimes.com/2021/08/04/us/politics/nsa-public-wifi.html (accessed November 04, 2022).

Yee, A. April 29, 2022. "4 Ways to Stay Safe on Public Wi-Fi." *PCWorld.* www.pcworld.com/article/693643/4-things-you-should-do-to-stay-safe-on-public-wi-fi.html (accessed November 29, 2022).

Chapter 15

Andriotis, A.M. and E. Glazer. September 26, 2017. "Equifax CEO Richard Smith to Exit Following Massive Data Breach." *The Wall Street Journal.* www.wsj.com/articles/equifax-ceo-richard-smith-to-retire-following-massive-data-breach-1506431571?mod=article_inline (accessed December 05, 2022).

Axelrod, T. April 03, 2019. "Warren Introduces Legislation Making It Easier to Jail Top Executives." *The Hill.* https://thehill.com/homenews/senate/437128-warren-introduces-legislation-making-it-easier-to-jail-top-business/ (accessed December 07, 2022).

Forbes. July 1, 2002. "WorldCom, Tyco, Enron—R.I.P." *Forbes.* www.forbes. com/2002/07/01/0701topnews.html?sh=69b43f245397 (accessed December 06, 2022).

Fritz, B. February 05, 2015. "Amy Pascal Steps Down as Head of Sony's Film Business." *The Wall Street Journal.* www.wsj.com/articles/amy-pascal-steps-down-as-head-of-sony-pictures-film-business-1423157351?mod=article_ inline (accessed December 05, 2022).

King & Spalding. July 15, 2021. "SEC Returns Spotlight to Cybersecurity Disclosure Enforcement." *JD Supra.* www.jdsupra.com/legalnews/sec-returns-spotlight-to-cybersecurity-6982863/ (accessed December 07, 2022).

Matsuo, A.S. n.d. "Cybersecurity: SEC Proposals for Public Company Reporting, Disclosures." *KPMG Advisory Services.* KPMG. https://advisory.kpmg.us/ articles/2022/sec-cybersecurity-disclosures-reg-alert-mar-2022.html (accessed December 12, 2022).

Newman, L.H. September 14, 2017. "The Equifax Breach Was Entirely Preventable." *Wired.* www.wired.com/story/equifax-breach-no-excuse/ (accessed December 06, 2022).

Roberts, D. July 10, 2015. "OPM Director Resigns over Data Hack That Affected up to 22 Million Americans." *The Guardian.* www.theguardian.com/ technology/2015/jul/10/opm-hack-director-katherine-archuleta-resigns (accessed December 05, 2022).

Rundle, J. April 15, 2022. "Boards, Security Chiefs Face Challenges Over New Cyber Rules." *The Wall Street Journal.* WSJ. www.wsj.com/articles/boards-security-chiefs-face-challenges-over-new-cyber-rules-11650015001?page=1 &mod=djemCybersecruityPro&tpl=cy (accessed December 08, 2022).

Turgal, J. June 07, 2022. "New SEC Cybersecurity Rules Focus on Board Accountability." *NACD BoardTalk.* NACD BoardTalk. https://blog.nacdonline. org/posts/sec-cybersecurity-board-accountability (accessed December 08, 2022).

U.S. Securities and Exchange Commission. 2018. *Commission Statement and Guidance on Public Company Cybersecurity Disclosures.* www.sec.gov/rules/ interp/2018/33-10459.pdf.

U.S. Securities and Exchange Commission. March 09, 2022. "Fact Sheet: Public Company Cybersecurity; Proposed Rules." www.sec.gov/files/33-11038-fact-sheet.pdf.

U.S. Securities and Exchange Commission. March 09, 2022. "SEC Proposes Rules on Cybersecurity Risk Management, Strategy, Governance, and Incident Disclosure by Public Companies." U.S. Securities and Exchange Commission. www.sec.gov/news/press-release/2022-39?utm_source=newsletter&utm_ medium=email&utm_campaign=newsletter_axioscodebook&stream=top.

U.S. Securities and Exchange Commission. March 09, 2022. "SEC Proposed Rules: Cybersecurity Risk Management, Strategy, Governance, and Incident Disclosure." www.sec.gov/rules/proposed/2022/33-11038.pdf.

U.S. Securities and Exchange Commission Division of Enforcement. 2020. *Annual Report*. www.sec.gov/files/enforcement-annual-report-2020.pdf.

U.S. Securities and Exchange Commission Office of Compliance Inspections and Examinations. 2020. *Cybersecurity and Resiliency Observations*. www.sec.gov/files/OCIE%20Cybersecurity%20and%20Resiliency%20Observations.pdf.

Ziobro, P., M. Langley, and J.S. Lublin. May 05, 2014. "Target's Problem: Tar-Zhay Isn't Working." *The Wall Street Journal*. www.wsj.com/articles/target-replaces-ceo-steinhafel-following-massive-holiday-breach-13992 91072?tesla=y&mod=article_inline (accessed December 05, 2022).

Chapter 16

Barr, A. December 27, 2021. "5 Ways Social Media Impacts Cybersecurity." *eWEEK*. www.eweek.com/security/social-media-cybersecurity/ (accessed December 04, 2022).

Benjamin, R. September 04, 2014. "Tone at the Top—Today's Biggest Cyber-Security Weakness." *EForensics*. https://eforensicsmag.com/tone-at-the-top-todays-biggest-cyber-security-weakness-by-rob-benjamin/ (accessed December 09, 2022).

Bogna, J. January 14, 2022. "Don't Plug It In! How to Prevent a USB Attack." *PCMag*. www.pcmag.com/how-to/dont-plug-it-in-how-to-prevent-a-usb-attack (accessed October 04, 2022).

Gupta, A. April 16, 2020. "How to Handle Data Security with Offshore Teams." *Colocation America*. www.colocationamerica.com/blog/data-security-with-offshore-teams (accessed December 03, 2022).

Hendrickson, A. March 27, 2018. "The Dangers of Oversharing on Social Media." *About Manchester*. https://aboutmanchester.co.uk/the-dangers-of-oversharing-on-social-media/ (accessed December 04, 2022).

Lee, A., and J. Pudelek. May 13, 2020. "Tips for Good Cyber Hygiene." *Fermilab at Work*. https://news.fnal.gov/2020/05/tips-for-good-cyber-hygiene/ (accessed January 08, 2023).

Menders, D. October 03, 2019. "The Importance of Data Encryption in Cybersecurity." *TechWell*. www.techwell.com/techwell-insights/2019/10/importance-data-encryption-cybersecurity#:~:text=%20The%20Importance%20of%20Data%20Encryption%20in%20Cybersecurity,sensitive%20data.%20The%20installation%20and%20use...%20More%20 (accessed December 10, 2022).

Minder, K. November 29, 2022. "Good Cyber Hygiene Is a Civic Duty." *Inc. Com*. www.inc.com/kurtis-minder/good-cyber-hygiene-is-a-civic-duty.html (accessed December 09, 2022).

Patel, D. May 19, 2020. "The Dangers of Sharing Personal Information on Social Media." *Penn Today*. https://penntoday.upenn.edu/news/dangers-sharing-personal-information-social-media (accessed December 04, 2022).

Rundle, J. and C. Stupp. September 03, 2020. "Chief Executives Face Rising Accountability for Cyber Lapses." *The Wall Street Journal.* www.wsj.com/articles/chief-executives-face-rising-accountability-for-cyber-lapses-11599125400 (accessed December 09, 2022).

Siegel, D. July 07, 2021. "[Opinion] How Poor Password Hygiene Crippled Colonial Pipeline." *Pipeline Technology Journal.* www.pipeline-journal.net/news/opinion-how-poor-password-hygiene-crippled-colonial-pipeline (accessed December 09, 2022).

Sjouwerman, S. March 07, 2022. "Why Training Is Essential to Building a Strong Cybersecurity Culture." *Fast Company.* www.fastcompany.com/90723595/why-training-is-essential-to-building-a-strong-cybersecurity-culture (accessed December 11, 2022).

Stackpole, B. May 15, 2022. "How to Build a Culture of Cybersecurity." *MIT Sloan.* https://mitsloan.mit.edu/ideas-made-to-matter/how-to-build-a-culture-cybersecurity (accessed December 11, 2022).

Stone, M. March 29, 2022. "National Backup Day: Don't Forget the Basics." *Security Intelligence.* https://securityintelligence.com/articles/national-backup-day-remember-basics/ (accessed December 09, 2022).

Suer, M.F. October 18, 2018. "Shadow IT: The CIO's Perspective." *CIO.* www.cio.com/article/222428/shadow-it-the-cio-s-perspective.html (accessed December 03, 2022).

Tech Accord. August 31, 2020. "Basic Cyber Hygiene: The Importance of Patching." https://cybertechaccord.org/basic-cyber-hygiene-the-importance-of-patching/ (accessed December 09, 2022).

Thompson, M. June 28, 2021. "Why Cyber-Savvy Boards Are a Necessity." *Keyfactor.* www.keyfactor.com/blog/cyber-savvy-boards-top-security-trends/ (accessed December 19, 2022).

Tunggal, A. Nov 22, 2022. "What is an Attack Vector? 16 Common Attack Vectors in 2022." *UpGuard Blog.* https://www.upguard.com/blog/attack-vector (accessed January 08, 2023).

Zongo, P. October 29, 2021. "Four Levers to Drive a Cyber-Savvy Culture." *ISACA.* www.isaca.org/resources/news-and-trends/isaca-now-blog/2021/four-levers-to-drive-a-cyber-savvy-culture (accessed December 19, 2022).

About the Author

Frank Riccardi, JD, CHC, is a cybersecurity and privacy expert and former C-level executive with 25 years of experience developing compliance and privacy programs for large healthcare systems comprised of hospitals, physician practice groups, urgent care centers, outpatient clinical laboratories, diagnostic imaging centers, and managed care organizations.

Riccardi has held positions as Chief Compliance and Privacy Officer overseeing high-profile data breaches and cybersecurity investigations. Areas of specialization include cybersecurity, data privacy, health information technology, and healthcare law.

Riccardi earned his JD from the Western New England University School of Law, a BS in clinical laboratory sciences from the State University of New York at Stony Brook, and is certified in healthcare compliance by the Compliance Certification Board (CCB).

Index

OTHER TITLES IN THE BUSINESS LAW AND CORPORATE RISK MANAGEMENT COLLECTION

- *Enhanced Enterprise Risk Management* by John Sidwell and Peter Hlavnicka
- *A Corporate Librarian's Guide to Information Governance and Data Privacy* by Phyllis L. Elin
- *A Government Librarian's Guide to Information Governance and Data Privacy* by Phyllis Elin and Max Rapaport
- *Protecting the Brand, Volume II* by Peter Hlavnicka and Anthony M. Keats
- *Can. Trust. Will.* by Leeza Garber and Scott Olson
- *Protecting the Brand, Volume I* by Peter Hlavnicka and Anthony M. Keats
- *Business Sustainability* by Zabihollah Rezaee
- *Business Sustainability Factors of Performance, Risk, and Disclosure* by Zabihollah Rezaee
- *The Gig Mafia* by David M. Shapiro
- *Guerrilla Warfare in the Corporate Jungle* by K. F. Dochartaigh
- *Consumer Protection in E-Retailing in ASEAN* by Huong Ha
- *A Book About Blockchain* by Rajat Rajbhandari

Concise and Applied Business Books

The Collection listed above is one of 30 business subject collections that Business Expert Press has grown to make BEP a premiere publisher of print and digital books. Our concise and applied books are for...

- Professionals and Practitioners
- Faculty who adopt our books for courses
- Librarians who know that BEP's Digital Libraries are a unique way to offer students ebooks to download, not restricted with any digital rights management
- Executive Training Course Leaders
- Business Seminar Organizers

Business Expert Press books are for anyone who needs to dig deeper on business ideas, goals, and solutions to everyday problems. Whether one print book, one ebook, or buying a digital library of 110 ebooks, we remain the affordable and smart way to be business smart. For more information, please visit www.businessexpertpress.com, or contact sales@businessexpertpress.com.